AN UNLIKELY
SUCCESS STORY

This view of the Lagan c. 1911 shows the Harland and Wolff yard, and the south yard of Workman Clark, on the left. The north yard of Workman Clark is on the right. In the foreground is the Thompson dry dock with the entrance to the Alexandra dry dock just beyond.

AN UNLIKELY SUCCESS STORY

THE BELFAST SHIPBUILDING INDUSTRY

1880–1935

J.P. LYNCH

THE BELFAST SOCIETY

IN ASSOCIATION WITH

THE ULSTER HISTORICAL FOUNDATION

First published 2001
by the Belfast Society, c/o Linen Hall Library,
17 Donegall Square North, Belfast BT1 5GD
in association with the Ulster Historical Foundation
12 College Square East, Belfast BT1 6DD

Distributed by
the Ulster Historical Foundation

© J.P. Lynch
ISBN 0-9539604-3-9

Printed by ColourBooks Ltd
Design by Dunbar Design

For my parents

who taught me both to value work
and respect the worker

CONTENTS

ACKNOWLEDGEMENTS

I WOULD LIKE TO THANK Ken Brown and Liam Kennedy who acted as supervisors for my doctoral thesis on which this book is based and Alan Reid who acted as my external examiner. I would also like to acknowledge the help and assistance of other members of staff in the Department of Economic and Social History at the Queen's University of Belfast, particularly the late Dave Johnson and Valerie Fawcett, the Departmental Secretary.

I would like to record my thanks to the staff at the Queen's University Library, the Linen Hall Library, Belfast Central Library and the Public Record Office of Northern Ireland where the research for this publication was undertaken. I also wish to express my thanks to Angélique Day and Eileen Black of the Belfast Society for their patience and invaluable support in this project and the latter in particular for her editorial comments on the text.

Illustrations on pages 1 and 5 are from Workman, Clark & Co. *The shipbuilding and engineering works of Workman, Clark and Co, Ltd: shipbuilders and engineers, Belfast, Ireland.* (Belfast, McCaw, Stevenson & Orr, 1902).

The illustrations on pages 52, 54, 58 and 59 are from Workman Clark (1928) Ltd. *Shipbuilding at Belfast 1880–1933.* (London, Cheltenham, published for Workman Clark (1928) Ltd, 1934).

The illustration on page 7 is from C.C. Pounder, *Some notable Belfast-built engines* (Belfast, Belfast Association of Engineers, 1948).

The cover, frontispiece and illustrations on pages 10, 12, 16, 30, 36 and 43 are reproduced with the kind permission of the Trustees of the Ulster Museum Belfast.

The south yard of Workman Clark, formerly that of McIlwaine and McColl, c. 1903, a good illustration of the crowded and dangerous conditions in a contemporary shipyard. This one was unusually well equipped, with a standard-gauge railway line running through the yard and narrow-gauge lines connecting the building slips with the various departments

1

ORIGINS
OF AN INDUSTRY

OWING TO ITS SURVIVAL, and some impressive self-publicity, the story of shipbuilding in Belfast is often portrayed as the story of Harland and Wolff.[1] However, for much of its history the industry consisted of two major producers and, for a considerable period, three. This account aims to offer a view of the industry as a whole rather than the successful survivor of the inter-war depression. Edward Harland and Gustav Wolff may have founded the Belfast shipbuilding industry in 1858 but, by the end of the 1870s, the engineering firm of MacIlwaine and Lewis was building ships in the Abercorn Basin and, in 1879, a third shipyard was opened by Frank Workman and George Clark.

By the start of the twentieth century Belfast had become one of the main centres of the British shipbuilding industry and, in some years before the First World War, the city's yards were producing up to 10%

of British merchant shipping output.[2] The success of the industry is a matter of historical fact but in the 1830s, when factory-based linen production was beginning to transform Belfast from a commercial centre to an industrial town, the location offered little to attract a shipbuilder. Unlike Cork or Dublin, there was only a very limited tradition of wooden shipbuilding, from which modern iron or steel construction might have developed. The Lagan, upon which Belfast stands, was totally unsuited for large-scale shipbuilding until massive improvements were undertaken in the 1840s. The city could offer a reservoir of cheap unskilled labour, which, in the view of Pollard and Robertson, was of great importance.[3] However, shipbuilding depended upon skilled labour, a commodity which was not available in Belfast, or even in Ireland, and which therefore had to be recruited from other areas.

Even after the Lagan was dredged and straightened to form the Victoria Channel in the 1840s, it was far from ideal as a site for the construction of large vessels, being even more congested and restricted than the Thames, where such constraints are frequently blamed for the decline of shipbuilding on that river. There were few local customers for the yards, as Belfast, although dependent on imported raw materials and export markets for its manufactures, was not a major shipowning centre. Inclusive of yachts, ferries and lighters, there were only 274 steamers with a combined tonnage of 72,248 and 123 sailing craft of 43,310 tons registered in the city in 1889, of which only forty-two were over 1,000 tons and the average was a mere 381.[4] Dependence on external customers was not a factor unique to the Belfast shipyards, but was to have political repercussions in later years, when Unionists argued that Home Rule would deprive the industry of its markets.

The disadvantages under which Belfast shipbuilders laboured become clearer when comparisons are drawn with other major shipbuilding centres at this time. The shipyards of the Clyde, Barrow and the north-east were all situated near coal and iron supplies, which gave them a cost advantage compared to the Lagan.[5] The cost of importing such commodities might appear unimportant in a high value-added industry such as shipbuilding, but anything that added to overheads in this highly competitive sector was a significant disadvantage. The only other major centre which shared Belfast's poverty of resources was Birkenhead, but there Cammell Laird enjoyed proximity to the largest shipping centre in Britain, Liverpool. On balance, competition from other well-established centres, combined with local limitations, should have precluded the development of shipyards in Belfast. How, therefore, in the face of such considerable disadvantages, did the town develop into one of the world's great shipbuilding centres? The answer to this question has been presented at various times as happy coincidence of timing, luck, nepotism or the Protestant work ethic.[6] Attractive as these reasons may be, none adequately explains the phenomenal growth of the Belfast shipyards in the fifty years before the First World War. A major cause of this expansion was the rapid adaptation of the Belfast shipyards to the technological revolution within the industry created by the adoption of iron and later steel hulls and steam propulsion. Belfast was one of a number of centres with little or no tradition of shipbuilding, which developed at this time largely on the basis of 'new technology'. Other British examples include Barrow and the Hartlepools.[7]

When the Belfast Harbour Commissioners equipped a new shipyard in 1853, at a cost of £1,116 17s 6d they included equipment for shaping and boring iron plates and angles; thus from its inception, the yard was intended to build iron rather than wooden vessels.[8] The young Edward Harland developed this initial 'high tech' investment after he acquired the yard in 1858. In common with a number of other centres, the shipyards were situated on reclaimed land located next to artificial deep-water channels. In the case of Belfast the improvements in port facilities were not just a necessary precondition for the establishment of a modern shipbuilding industry, but actually created the land on which it was established.[9] The Belfast Harbour Commissioners were responsible for these improvement schemes, and laid out the first shipyard to encourage the use of reclaimed land. Although relations between the Commissioners and the shipbuilders were not always harmonious, the importance of co-operation was fully acknowledged.

'We have never built a ship', Pirrie informed the Clyde Navigation Trust in 1922, 'that the Harbour Commissioners of Belfast had not built a graving dock ready to accommodate that vessel the day we launched her'.[10]

The attitude of the Belfast Harbour Commissioners contrasts with that of the authorities in Liverpool, where powerful shipowning and dock interests, which controlled the harbour authority effectively, forced shipbuilding out of the city. Liverpool shipowners were compelled to place their orders elsewhere, frequently in Belfast. So important was this connection to become that various contemporaries nicknamed the Lagan the 'Shipyard of the Mersey'.

After Edward Harland took over the Belfast yard in 1858 his first orders, gained through family connections, were from the Liverpool-based firm of John Bibby and Sons. Some of these early ships, such as the *Grecian* and *Italian* were built using the most advanced methods, as Harland later recalled:

> I was allowed to settle the dimensions; and the following were decided upon: length 310 feet; beam 34 feet; depth of hold 24 feet 9 inches; all of which were fully compensated for by making the upper deck entirely of iron ... in this way the hull was converted into a box girder of immensely increased strength.[11]

The increased hull length and structural strength made possible by such innovations allowed a considerable increase in cargo and passenger carrying capacity. These developments resulted in ships whose solid-box-like appearance earned them the nickname of 'Bibby coffins'. Despite the rather unpleasant connotation, Harland's iron 'coffin ships' proved highly popular with owners, ensuring his initial success in a highly competitive market.

This was of particular importance as the Belfast shipyards had to raise capital by share sales or loans. None of the yards were part of larger industrial groupings that would have allowed them to benefit from internal investment and the individuals establishing the yards were not sufficiently wealthy to fund such developments. In the circumstances it can be argued that a full order book was necessary to attract the investment needed to develop the yards rather than investment attracting orders.

From its beginning in the late 1850s, the Belfast shipbuilding industry was notable for its state-of-the-art design and construction methods. In part at least this was a strategy to allow the yards to compete with longer established but more conservative rivals in other regions. The use of steel in the building of ships' hulls began in the following decade, when it was used in specially built blockade-runners such as the *Banshee* during the American Civil War (1861–65). In these highly specialised vessels, steel was used to reduce hull weight, thus allowing increased speed and shallow draught without

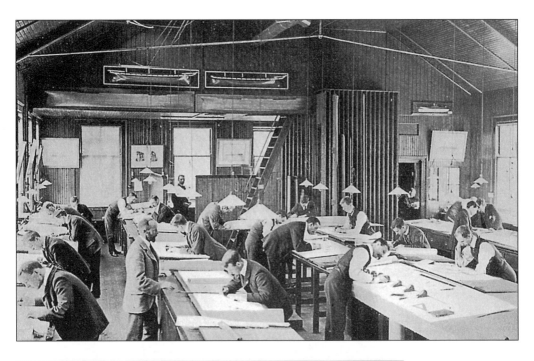

ABOVE
The drawing office
in Workman Clark's
north yard, c. 1903.

A corner of the
model shop at
Workman Clark.
Edwardian shipyards
modelled every vessel
exactly to scale
before starting
construction, in
order to discover any
problems in the
design.

sacrificing structural strength.[12]   However, steel was to remain too expensive to compete with iron for routine shipbuilding use until the widespread adoption of the Bessemer and open-hearth processes substantially lowered prices at the end of the 1870s. The first ocean going steel-hulled ship, the *Rotomahana*, was built by William Denny and Co. on the Clyde in 1879. This new technology was quickly adopted in Belfast, where Harland and Wolff launched the steel-hulled sister ships *British King* and *British Queen* at the end of 1880.[13] Workman Clark first used steel in the construction of the *Teelin Head* in 1883,[14] whilst even the small yard of MacIlwaine and Lewis were building their colliers in steel rather than iron by 1887.[15] The state-of-the-art nature of this development is shown by the fact that as late as 1882 there were only twenty steel-hulled steamers and three sailing vessels on Lloyd's register.

Although more difficult to work than iron, a steel hull could be up to 15% lighter than an iron one, a saving which allowed the Belfast yards rapidly to increase the size of ship they produced. When the first liner built by Harland and Wolff for the White Star Line, the iron-hulled *Oceanic* of 1871, is compared with the *Titanic*, built for the same customer in 1912, the extent of technical advance becomes clear. Both vessels were 'liners' and represented the very peak of marine technology on their completion.

FIGURE 1
Comparative data *Oceanic* (1871) and *Titanic* (1912)[16]

	Oceanic	*Titanic*
Length (feet)	420	882.5
Gross tonnage	3,808	42,238
Horsepower	3,000	46,000
Speed (knots)	14.75	21
Hull material	iron	steel
Engines	compound	reciprocating and exhaust turbines

Compared to other centres, Belfast's shipbuilding industry was notable for the fact that there were only two or three firms in the city, compared to forty-five on the Clyde and seventeen on the Wear; also, that the average size of ship produced was the largest in Britain.[17]

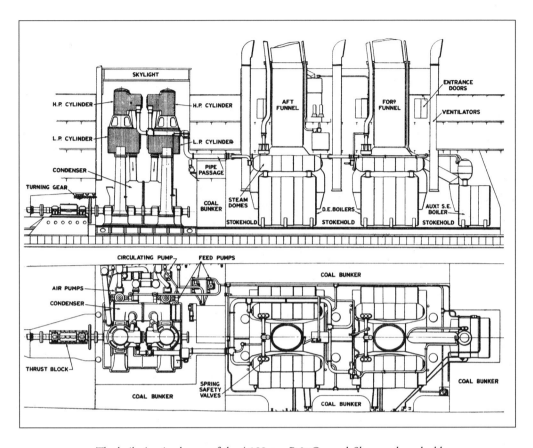

The boiler/engine layout of the 4,189-ton P & O vessel *Shannon*, launched by Harland and Wolff in October 1881. She was powered by compound engines, a type shortly to be superseded by triple-expansion engines.

In marine engineering the Belfast yards were also innovators, for at the same time as steel was being adopted for hull construction, the triple expansion engine was replacing earlier compound types. An early form of triple expansion was used in the *Arizona* of 1879 and the fully developed engine was installed in the Armstrong-built cruiser *Dogali* of 1884.[18] Once again, Belfast's shipbuilders quickly adopted this new technology, with Harland and Wolff beginning to construct such engines from 1885.[19] Harland and Wolff in the *Laurentic* of 1908 pioneered the system employed on the *Titanic*, the linking of two low-pressure exhaust turbines to high-pressure reciprocating engines.[20] In the same year, the company began working on the development of marine diesels with the Danish firm of Burmeister and Wain.[21] In 1905 Workman Clark delivered the *Victorian,* the first turbine-driven mail steamer in service on the north Atlantic route, to the firm of J & A Allen.[22] After the war, Workman Clark were also to build the first British vessel to employ turbo-electric propulsion, the *San Benito* of 1921.[23]

The origins of commercially successful shipbuilding in Belfast stem from late 1854, when Edward James Harland arrived in Belfast to manage a small struggling shipyard operated by Robert Hickson. Harland did not intend his stay in the town to be a lengthy one:

> He [Edward Harland] soon planned to set up on his own and in 1857 applied to Liverpool City Council for ground at Garstang to build a shipyard there, but he was turned down because of his 'youth and inexperience'. Further applications at Birkenhead and elsewhere on the Mersey were also rejected.[24]

Had he been successful in obtaining a yard in Liverpool, the history of the Belfast shipbuilding industry could have been very different; however, it would be wrong to credit the success of the industry solely to Harland, despite his considerable gifts. In 1857 he engaged Gustav Wilhelm Wolff, the nephew of Gustav Christian Schwabe, an old friend of his family, as his personal assistant. Wolff, a trained engineer and draughtsman, brought to the partnership not only his own particular skills but also another important asset – the support of his uncle. This was of considerable importance as Schwabe, amongst his other business activities, owned the Liverpool-based shipping firm of John Bibby and Sons.

> Harland's decision to acquire the lease of the Queen's Island yard was almost certainly taken on Schwabe's advice and promise of financial support, for immediately John Bibby & Sons placed an order for three 1,500-gross-ton iron steamers.[25]

As already mentioned, these ships were built to Harland's own design and were the first of the highly successful 'coffin ships' which were to establish his reputation as a builder in a highly competitive industry. Schwabe's family ties with Wolff ensured the early success of the new company. This can be seen by the construction list, which shows that of the first fifteen vessels built by Harland, twelve were ordered by the Bibby Line. More importantly, in terms of tonnage, out of 18,552 launched, only 1,026 (5.5%) went to other customers.[26] This family connection was vital in the firm's early days but could only be a short-term advantage, as a single shipping line could not generate enough work to keep the yard in full production.

A major factor in the long-term success of Harland and Wolff in Belfast was timing: the firm was fortunate enough to finish the last Bibby ship when demand for shipping was at a peak. The American Civil War of 1861–65, whilst creating severe depression in a number of areas of the British economy, caused a boom in the Belfast linen industry which benefited from disruption in cotton supplies and stimulated demand for shipping. Although it has been suggested that Harland built blockade-runners for the Confederacy, the building list does not support this claim.[27] After the completion of the last Bibby vessel, the company went through a period of extremely varied production. Of twenty-eight vessels delivered in the period between October 1862 and December 1865, sixteen were sailing vessels and seven were tugs or other harbour or river craft. Harland and Wolff benefited from the high level of demand within the British shipbuilding industry as a whole, both for war-related activities such as blockade-running and to allow British ship owners to replace American operators driven from the seas by Confederate cruisers. Harland and Wolff successfully broadened their customer base, these vessels being completed for no fewer than nineteen customers, some of whom developed into regular clients.[28]

Again, personal and family contacts were often critical in the development of these business relationships. According to popular legend, it was during an after-dinner game of billiards at Schwabe's Liverpool home in 1869 that Edward Harland met Thomas Ismay and obtained one of the most important orders in his company's history. That evening, Harland was supposed to have agreed to build the ships Ismay needed to allow his newly-acquired White Star Line to compete in the north-Atlantic emigrant trade. The game of billiards, if it took place, was to affect the Belfast shipbuilding industry profoundly.[29]

> To meet an immediate order for five 420 foot vessels at over £110,000 each, with the novel feature of financial penalty for late delivery, Harland and Wolff had to re-equip the yard completely at a cost of £30,000 … The *Oceanic,* the first White Star ship to be

Harland and Wolff's yard before the First World War. Everything about this scene, from the clutter around the building slip to the flimsy handrails on the ramps leading to the upper deck, shows that safety was not the major consideration. Injury and death were common occurrences.

launched at Queen's Island, can be regarded as the first modern liner.[30]

With this undertaking, Harland and Wolff established themselves as builders of passenger vessels of the highest quality, a product which was to become their speciality in future years. By 1880, therefore, Belfast had firmly established its reputation as a centre for shipbuilding; furthermore the founding firm was beginning to attract competitors, as the following chapter will show.

NOTES

1   Moss and Hume, *Shipbuilders.*
2   Geary and Johnson, 'Shipbuilding', p. 48.
3   Pollard and Robertson, *Shipbuilding*, pp. 66–7.
4   Vance, *The Belfast Shipping List*, pp. 15–22.
5   Moss and Hume, *Workshop*, pp. 11–26; Dougan, *North East shipbuilding*, pp. 35, 62–3; Pollard and Robertson, *Shipbuilding*, pp. 67–8.
6   Moss and Hume, *Shipbuilders*, pp. 11–35.
7   Pollard and Robertson, *Shipbuilding*, p. 49.
8   Moss and Hume, *Shipbuilders*, p. 12.
9   Pollard and Robertson, *Shipbuilding*, pp. 510–11.
10 Ibid., p. 66.
11 Ibid., p. 19.
12 Wise, *Lifeline of the Confederacy*, pp. 112–3.
13 Moss and Hume, *Shipbuilders*, pp. 46–7.
14 Workman Clark, *Shipbuilding*, 'Particulars of vessels built'; *Lloyds Register of Shipping* (1892).
15 Lynch, 'Belfast's Third Shipyard', p. 24.
16 Dyos, H.J. and Aldcroft, D.H., *British transport*, p. 244; Ulster Folk and Transport Museum, *Olympic/Titanic publicity booklet*, p. 5.
17 Pollard and Robertson, *Shipbuilding*, p. 49.
18 Moss and Hume, *Workshop*, p. 39; Dougan, *North East shipbuilding*, p. 69.
19 Pounder, *Belfast-built engines*, p. 15.
20 Moss and Hume, *Shipbuilders*, pp. 133–5; Pounder, *Belfast–built engines*, pp. 21–5.
21 Moss and Hume, *Shipbuilders*, pp. 155; Pounder, *Belfast-built engines*, pp. 21–5.
22 Coe, *Engineering industry*, p. 86; Workman Clark, *Shipbuilding*, p. 46.
23 Workman Clark, *Shipbuilding*, p. 46.
24 Bardon, *History of Ulster*, p. 335.
25 Moss and Hume, *Shipbuilders*, p. 18.
26 Ibid., p. 507.
27 Bardon, *History of Ulster*, p. 335.
28 Moss and Hume, *Shipbuilders*, pp. 510–11.
29 Ibid., pp. 28–9.
30 Bardon, *History of Ulster*, p. 337.

Given the size of most ships constructed by the Belfast yards, hand riveting was impractical for the heavier steel work and both yards adopted hydraulic machinery to perform this task. The great gantry erected over slips 1 and 2 in Harland and Wolff's yard was the most dramatic example of this technology. Workman Clark employed different but equally effective methods.

2

THE
GOLDEN AGE
1880–1914

THE YEARS BETWEEN THE ESTABLISHMENT of Workman Clark in 1879 and the outbreak of the First World War were to see massive growth in Belfast's shipbuilding industry. The Belfast yards developed a specialism in large vessels, the average for Belfast-built ships being 1,180 tons between 1867 and 1872 and 3,960 between 1907 and 1913. In contrast, figures for the Clyde were 640 and 1,260 and for the Wear 530 and 2,030.[1] The building lists show the reasons for this. Harland and Wolff and Workman Clark concentrated on the production of passenger liners, cargo-passenger ships and large ocean-going cargo vessels. They built very few coasters, ferries, tugs, fishing craft or small warships, which would have reduced the average size of vessel produced. As Pollard and Robertson point out, this concentration on large ocean going vessels represents a survival strategy within a highly competitive industry allowing the Belfast yards to compete with other centres despite their natural disadvantages.[2]

HARLAND AND WOLFF

By 1879, Harland and Wolff were one of the United Kingdom's major shipbuilders. From 1884 William Pirrie, who had become a partner ten years before, effectively controlled the firm. The yard specialised increasingly in high quality passenger vessels (see Figure 2). To ensure sufficient orders for these Pirrie used a system, which became known as the 'Commission Club'. This had first been adopted in the firm's dealings with the White Star Line but was thereafter made available to other customers.[3] Under this particular system, the customer paid the actual cost of construction plus a proportion of the yard's overheads, the firm's profit being fixed at 5% of the final figure. The profit on such business may have been lower than might have been obtained under other conditions

FIGURE 2

Ship production Harland and Wolff 1880–1914

	A	B	C	D	E	F	G	H	TOTAL
1880–4	9	21		2		5	2	1	40
1885–9	10	25	2			4	6	2	49
1890–4	3	32	5	1		21	2	3	67
1895–9		10	1	7		23	1		42
1900–4		2				29	2		33
1905–9	1	20		4		15	4		44
1910–14		1		13		12	1	2	29
TOTAL	23	111	8	27	0	109	18	8	304
% OF TOTAL	7.5	36.0	2.5	9.0	0	36.0	6.0	2.5	

A = sailing ships, B = cargo ships, C = specialist cargo ships,
D = passenger/cargo ships, E = specialist passenger/cargo ships,
F = passenger ships, G = Miscellaneous vessels including warships,
H = lighter, barge etc.

but the 'club' linked ship owners to Harland and Wolff by a network of shared self-interest. There was also an increasingly complex system of mutual shareholdings and directorships between shipbuilder and customer, culminating in 1902 when Harland and Wolff became part of the International Merchant Marine Syndicate. Under the terms of this agreement, Harland's were to receive all orders for new vessels from the member companies which they would build at preferential rates, in addition to undertaking any heavy repair work to be carried out within the United Kingdom.[4] As a result of these methods, Pirrie was able to secure sufficient high quality work of the type which the yard specialised in, although orders tended to be dominated by a small group of companies (see Figure 3). In contrast, fewer than twenty vessels were built for operators who did not place further orders for ships during these years. This 'customer loyalty' was of critical importance to the survival of both the main Belfast shipyards.

If Harland and Wolff were to continue to build huge liners, they had to obtain a continuous supply of work to allow them to retain irreplaceable skilled workers. The 'Commission Club' and similar 'arrangements' made it possible for the firm to insulate its labour force from fluctuations in demand to a certain degree although periodic slumps were inevitable.[5] Between 1880 and 1914, Harland's yard was frequently expanded and re-equipped to meet the demand for ever larger and more luxurious passenger vessels. This is best illustrated by the vast gantry erected over No. 2 and 3 Slips, which allowed the simultaneous construction of the giant liners *Olympic* and *Titanic*.[6] However, by 1914, the workload of the firm had increased to the point where the Belfast yard was no longer adequate and the company was obliged to establish additional repair facilities in Liverpool and Southampton, as well as building yards on the Clyde.

FIGURE 3

Customers obtaining six or more vessels from Harland and Wolff 1880–1913[7]

OWNER	SHIPS	TONNAGE	YEARS ORDERED
Oceanic Steam Navigation	46	503,846	1880–1913
Union/Union Castle SS Co.	16	129,584	1893–1911
Hamburg Amerika Line	14	154,895	1894–1911
Pacific Steam Navigation Co.	14	94,193	1892–1913
Royal Mail Steam Packet Co.	14	124,499	1904–1913
F. Leyland and Co.	13	91,436	1888–1908
Bibby Steamship Co.	12	79,291	1889–1912
T. & J. Brocklebank	12	60,539	1885–1906
African Steamship Co.	10	30,386	1881–1912
Belfast Steamship Co.	9	12,246	1883–1912
Elder Dempster & Co.	8	32,179	1890–1907
Irish Shipowners Co.	8	24,672	1883–1892
Peninsular & Oriental SS	8	61,693	1880–1910
Asiatic Steamship Co.	7	24,217	1885–1892
Edward Bates & Sons	7	35,334	1886–1896
British Shipowners Ltd	7	23,050	1880–1891
West Indian and Pacific	6	29,971	1882–1896
TOTAL	211	1,519,940	
Firm's total output	302	2,003,476	
% TOTAL OUTPUT	69.9	75.9	

Although neither Harland and Wolff nor Workman Clark specialised in
warship construction and comparatively few Admiralty contracts were given to
the Belfast yards, both yards undertook repair and refit work and supplied engines
and equipment to the naval dockyards.
This particular vessel is the *St George*, a first class protected cruiser of
the Edger class completed in 1894.

WORKMAN CLARK

Although known in Belfast as the 'wee yard', Workman Clark was a
major shipbuilding firm and consistently amongst the top British
producers in terms of tonnage. The tensions between Harland and
Wolff and Workman Clark went beyond the normal rivalry between
two producers in a highly competitive industry. Frank Workman and
George Clark had trained as premium apprentices at Harland and
Wolff and were appointed to management positions within that firm.
As a result, they enjoyed a wide range of contacts amongst their former employer's customers and were able to 'steal' some of their business when they established their own yard in 1879. In addition, the
Workman family had ship-owning connections, whilst the Clarks
were significant figures in the Scottish and Ulster textile industries. As
with Harland and Wolff two decades before, these family connections

were of great significance in the early success of the yard.[8] The new firm opened a yard opposite Queen's Island and enjoyed more space and better facilities than its longer-established rival, notably their own fitting-out basin. Although at first their building list was fairly modest compared with Harland and Wolff's, they were soon producing substantial vessels of up to 4,500 tons.[9] Capacity was increased in 1893 when the firm acquired the Queen's Island yard of MacIlwaine and MacColl. The *Belfast Trades Directory* for 1896 contains an interesting passage on this acquisition:

> [Workman Clark] have also purchased the yard and engine works belonging to the firm of MacIlwaine and MacColl Ltd and thus have four separate establishments under their control. For the year 1893 they were 20th in the list of shipbuilders and for 1894 the sixth place. Thus demonstrating the great strides and growing importance of this young and enterprising firm.[10]

Although frequently presented as bitter rivals the two firms did not allow their mutual antagonism to interfere with profit; Harland and Wolff's papers indicate that communication between the yards could be amicable and even friendly. Co-operation was particularly noticeable during industrial disputes or on the question of rates of pay.[11] This co-operation was possible as Workman Clark specialised increasingly in smaller and less prestigious cargo and passenger/cargo ships, supplemented, from the beginning of the twentieth century, by refrigerated and chilled vessels for the meat and fruit trades.[12] Although both yards initially shared an interest in cargo vessels, as time went by their output tended to concentrate on different types of ship (see Figure 4), and had quite distinct lists of customers, thus eliminating any real competition.

FIGURE 4

Ship output of Specific Types 1880–1914[13]

	HARLAND AND WOLFF		WORKMAN CLARK	
	1880–1900	1900–1914	1880–1900	1900–1914
Cargo Vessels	48.5%	21.7%	59.4%	47.4%
Cargo/Passenger	5.0%	14.2%	10.6%	33.1%
Passenger	28.8%	52.8%	0.0%	6.3%

FIGURE 5

Ship production Workman Clark 1880–1914[14]

(Key see Figure 2)

	A	B	C	D	E	F	G	H	TOTAL
1880–4	6	19		3			2	3	33
1885–9	7	17		3			4	2	33
1890–4	17	24		3			2	2	48
1895–9	1	35		6	2			2	46
1900–4		33	3	8		1	1	7	53
1905–9		24	4	18	12	3	1	14	76
1910–4		19		11	9	7			46
TOTAL	31	171	7	52	23	11	10	30	335
% OF TOTAL	9%	51%	2%	15%	7%	3%	4%	9%	

Whilst Workman and Clark did not use the 'Commission Club' system employed by Pirrie, they nevertheless also built up a regular clientele. When the firm's building list is examined, a number of long-standing relationships become apparent (see Figure 6). If barges and small craft are excluded from the vessels built by the company between 1880 and 1913, 63% were built for customers who purchased six or more ships. In contrast, only forty-five vessels – 15% of total output – were produced for owners who did not subsequently order a further ship.[15] Such relationships between shipbuilder and owner were typical of British shipyards in these years and served to protect producers in a highly volatile market; thus in this matter Workman Clark were more typical of the industry generally than Harland and Wolff.

FIGURE 6

Customers obtaining six or more vessels from Workman Clark 1880–1913[16]

OWNER	SHIPS ORDERED	TONNAGE	YEARS ORDERED
Alfred Holt	28	182,908	1894–1913
United Fruit	19	98,037	1904–1913
J.P. Corry & Co	12	70,067	1886–1913
T. & J. Harrison	12	66,850	1891–1909
George Smith & Son	11	49,274	1882–1901

Lampton & Holt	9	59,676	1900–1913
Lloyds Brazilerio	9	25,704	1907–1909
Tysor & Co.	8	60,845	1900–1912
Allen Line	8	45,178	1893–1904
Houlder Bros	8	42,154	1895–1901
China Mutual SS Co.	8	41,162	1894–1902
Clark and Service	8	15,669	1883–1895
Elders Fyffe	7	32,221	1905–1913
Ulster SS Co.	7	27,692	1883–1913
Colvils, Lowden & Co.	7	5,187	1881–1890
Ellerman Line	6	40,759	1906–1913
W.J. Woodside	6	5,000	1884–1893
TOTAL	173	863,196	
FIRM'S TOTAL OUTPUT	310	1,271,000	
% TOTAL OUTPUT	55.8	67.9	

MacILWAINE AND PARTNERS

There is a tendency to discuss the history of shipbuilding in Belfast in terms of a single or at most two producers. However, during this period there was a third yard in operation, which at the time of its closure in 1894 had the potential to develop into a major producer.[17] The firm of MacIlwaine and Lewis was established in premises known as the Ulster Iron Works on the newly-opened Abercorn Basin in 1867. The company was listed as iron shipbuilders in the 1868 *Belfast Trades Directory* and in later years MacIlwaine was to claim this as the starting date for his company.[18] In fact, during the early years of the firm's existence, it operated as ship repairers rather than builders and it was not until 1876 that the company appeared to have launched their first vessel. This was the *Elizabeth Jane,* the first screw tug built in Belfast for the Lagan Canal Company. The firm was subsequently to built a number of iron barges for this customer, prior to the yard's expansion from one to four acres in 1880.[19]

The increase in the yard's size allowed the firm to extend their range of production. In 1880, their first vessel to merit inclusion in *Lloyd's List* the *Parkmore,* built for the Antrim Iron Ore Co., was launched. Although no building list survives, these years saw considerable activity. *Lloyd's List* shows that thirteen coasters, ferries and small cargo ships of between 108 and 456 tons were built, in addition to a number of vessels under 100 tons, plus barges and river craft.[20] Clearly, at this stage, MacIlwaine and Lewis were specialising in vessels at the smaller end of the market, rather than on the ocean-going ships of the other Belfast yards. However, as the shipping in Belfast harbour on the night of 3 April 1881 indicates, the demand for small coastal and river craft was considerable.

Vessels belonging to Local Boards and Corporation	68
Vessels in Foreign Trade	29
Vessels in Home or Coasting Trade	130
Fishing Vessels	6
Vessels engaged in Inland Navigation	42
Pleasure craft	44 [21]

Although the company had established a profitable niche in the market, John MacIlwaine appears to have been ambitious and keen to expand into other areas of production. In 1885 the original partnership was dissolved and MacIlwaine was joined by Hector MacColl. The new firm, established as a limited company, acquired an extensive yard next to Harland and Wolff in 1885 or 1886.[22] The improved facilities allowed the company to compete for orders for large sea-going ships, as well as increasing output, and over the next nine years the firm completed fifty-eight vessels.[23] Contemporary descriptions laid great stress on the firm's capacity to construct a wide range of shipping.[24] According to the *Belfast Trades Directory* of the time:

> [the firm] have built very fine ships for each department of the ship-building trade and furnished them with all the latest and most improved machinery of the day, and are in a position to turn out vessels of the largest type.[25]

A large proportion of their construction remained barges and small craft, as only twenty-three merited inclusion in *Lloyd's*. Of these, the majority were still small coasters and ferries, with only five of the vessels produced being over 1,000 tons.[26] Such a pattern of construction could not justify the heavy capital investment which had occurred in the new yard and serious financial problems resulted, which came to a head in 1893–94.

> Messrs MacIlwaine & MacColl Ltd, also built several steel steamers during 1893, but the firm has gone into liquidation, which is a

source of regret to all true friends of Belfast.[27]

The reason for MacIlwaine's failure lay in the cyclic nature of the British shipbuilding industry and the methods used to counter serious fluctuations in demand. By the 1890s, Harland and Wolff had established the 'Commission Club' and Workman Clark had created a regular clientele of customers. In both cases, these supplier/customer relationships guaranteed sufficient work in periods of slack demand. MacIlwaine and Co. also had a number of regular customers, notably the Cork, Passage and Blackrock Railway (four vessels) and the Belfast firms of William Granger (four vessels), J. Fisher and Sons (six vessels) and the Antrim Iron Ore Co. (four vessels). However, all these were relatively small-scale operators engaged in the cross-channel or coastal trade. Unlike the White Star or Royal Mail lines, these small customers could not generate sufficient work to keep the yard active in periods of depressed demand.

As already mentioned, MacIlwaine's yard and engine works were acquired by Workman Clark and John MacIlwaine returned to general engineering and ship repairing.[28] Of the legacy of this firm to the Belfast shipbuilding industry, their main contribution lies in the fact that their premises were of considerable importance to the expansion and later success of Workman Clark. Nevertheless, there is one distinction, which this short-lived yard can claim: it built the first Belfast *Titanic* (1,608 tons) for the Ulidian Steam Navigation Co. in 1888.[29]

RECRUITMENT OF SHIPBUILDING WORKERS 1880–1914

The greatest difficulty faced by Belfast's shipbuilders in these years was recruiting and retaining the skilled and diverse labour force needed to build iron and steel ships. In the 1850s, when shipbuilding began to develop, the city's main industry was linen, already employing over 15,000 people. The boom created by the American Civil War (1861–65) boosted employment to over 50,000 by 1870.[30] As 70% of those employed in the manufacture of linen were female, as was the case with the textile industries in general, there were more employment opportunities for women in Belfast than for men. The mills drew much of their semi-skilled female labour from eastern and central Ulster, where the tradition of linen manufacture was strongest. The city had a small engineering sector, mainly concerned with the manufacture and maintenance of textile machinery and other mill requirements, which provided limited skilled male employment. However, the shipyards required a highly-skilled male labour force which the town simply could not supply and in other areas of Ireland industrial, and particularly engineering, development was too limited to meet such a demand. The only means whereby a shipbuilder in Belfast could obtain skilled labour was to attract workers from the shipbuilding districts of Scotland and northern England.

This was not easy. Skilled workers were the element in the labour force who had the least reason to move as their skills were in demand in most British industrial centres at this time. Prejudice against Ireland and the Irish – and few differentiated between Ulster and other regions – was a feature of popular British culture.[31] The Irish were seen as comic but intrinsically violent by the inhabitants of British industrial cities. To an angle-iron smith from the Tyne or a boilermaker from the Mersey in the 1870s, Ireland was a foreign and hostile country. Belfast itself had an unenviable reputation and a ship-yard worker considering moving in 1870 might understandably have been discouraged by the city's reputation for sectarian violence.[32] From the point of view of employment, a newly-emerging district with only a single employer and few sources of alternative work could hardly have been an attractive proposition for skilled workers.

Why should a highly skilled and valued worker migrate from an established shipbuilding area to Belfast? The question is critical, for without such movement the shipyards of Belfast could not have sur-vived, let alone prospered as they did. In 1870, out of 2,400 men employed at the Queen's Island yard, 200 were said to be 'mechanics from London and Liverpool engaged in fitting machinery aboard ship'.[33] In the shipyard itself, trained labour from other centres was even more important throughout the early years of the industry.[34] When Harland and Wolff ceased to buy their propulsion machinery from contractors and built it themselves it was noticeable that the engine shop was nicknamed the 'English' works.

One of the most appealing factors may have been the scarcity value of skilled labour in Belfast, which consequently pushed up wage rates. However, the Belfast yards were not alone in expanding in these years – the same was occurring throughout the shipbuilding industry with the result that there was a shortage of skilled labour in most districts. Was this shortage more marked in Belfast than elsewhere? Pollard and

Robertson argue that Belfast wage rates were lower than other districts, with the exception of Barrow, which would suggest that this was not the case.[35] However, as late as 1905, there was a shortage of skilled labour in the city, as can be seen by rates of pay in the yards.

FIGURE 7

Inhabitants of Belfast of Scottish or English Birth

	POPULATION	ENGLISH OR SCOTTISH	ALL MALES	ALL FEMALE
		%	%	%
1861	121,602	5.1	n/a	n/a
1871	202,537	4.9	5.9	4.2
1881	239,280	4.9	5.4	4.5
1891	289,850	6.3	7.3	5.8
1901	349,180	6.7	7.1	6.3
1911	386,947	7.2	7.8	6.7 [36]

A feature often noted of Belfast at this time was the low cost of living compared to that found in many industrial cities in Britain. Employers, for example, frequently used this as an argument in favour of the payment of lower local wage rates than the nationally agreed standard.[37] By the 1890s, Belfast enjoyed two considerable housing advantages: the standard of accommodation was high and rents were low. Compared to the tenement flats of Glasgow, Greenock, Newcastle or South Shields, the 'kitchen' and 'parlour' houses of Belfast were positively luxurious. According to official statistics, only 8.2% of Belfast's population were living in overcrowded conditions in 1905; of the other shipbuilding centres, only Birkenhead with 5.02% could better this figure. Conversely, Barrow, Middlesborough and Stockton all exceeded 10%, whilst Newcastle, South Shields and Sunderland exceeded thirty.[38] When the standard of accommodation and levels of rent in Belfast are contrasted with other shipbuilding centres, a major advantage of living in the former becomes apparent: a Glaswegian worker could obtain a five-roomed house in Belfast for less than he would have paid for a three-roomed tenement in Glasgow.

FIGURE 8

Weekly Wages of Engineering Workers (October 1905)

	BELFAST	RANGE IN TEN OTHER SHIPBUILDING AREAS	AVERAGE OF OTHER AREAS
Fitter	37s	35-36s	35s 1d
Turner	38s	35-36s	35s 2d
Smith	37s	34-38s	35s 6d
Pattern Maker	39s	37-39s 6d	38s
Labourers	15-18s	18-23s 6d	approx. 20s[39]

Food prices were also believed to be lower in Ireland than in other industrial centres. If a Scottish or northern English worker moved to Belfast and did not wish to change his diet, how much would he have spent on food? A comparison can be made from statistics compiled by the Board of Trade for consumption of foodstuffs by workers earning thirty-five shillings per week.[40] When these are priced at 1905 levels for each shipbuilding centre, the results show considerable variation.

FIGURE 9

Percentage of Population (1901) living in

	1 ROOM	2 ROOM	3 ROOM	4 ROOM	5 ROOM+
Belfast	0.4	4.7	6.4	29.1	59.4
Barrow	0.6	8.6	7.2	12.1	71.5
Birkenhead	1.2	4.1	4.8	18.2	71.7
Glasgow	16.2	38.9	19.0	6.8	19.1
Greenock	11.3	47.6	21.4	6.5	13.2
Jarrow	3.3	31.0	24.5	18.9	22.3
Middlesborough	0.7	5.0	8.3	39.1	46.9
Newcastle	6.0	23.9	23.4	19.1	27.6
South Shields	4.3	31.5	23.5	19.5	21.2
Stockton	1.0	5.3	3.9	39.0	50.8
Sunderland	4.6	23.4	28.0	15.9	28.1 [41]

FIGURE 10

Rent Payable for Accommodation

	3 ROOMS		4 ROOMS	
	HIGHEST	LOWEST	HIGHEST	LOWEST
Belfast	3s 6d	2s 6d	5s 0d	3s 0d
Barrow	5s 6d	5s 0d	6s 0d	5s 6d
Birkenhead	6s 0d	4s 6d	7s 0d	6s 0d
Glasgow	7s 4d	6s 0d	not given	
Greenock	7s 0d	6s 0d	not given	
Jarrow	5s 9d	4s 9d	6s 9d	5s 3d
Middlesborough	4s 6d	3s 6d	6s 0d	4s 6d
Newcastle	6s 6d	5s 3d	7s 0d	6s 0d
South Shields	5s 9d	4s 0d	6s 6d	4s 6d
Stockton	4s 6d	3s 6d	5s 0d	4s 0d
Sunderland	5s 0d	3s 6d	7s 0d	5s 6d [42]

For a Scottish worker moving to Belfast, food was slightly cheaper, but in the case of English workers the cost was higher. However, if housing and food are taken together, then the standard of living was certainly higher for the skilled worker in Belfast. Was this sufficient inducement to attract skilled labour to the city?

FIGURE 11

Comparative Food Costs (1905)

	SCOTTISH DIET	ENGLISH DIET
Belfast	14s 3d	14s 10d
Barrow	14s 9d	14s 0d
Birkenhead	13s 10d	13s 6d
Glasgow	14s 7d	14s 4d
Greenock	15s 1d	14s 7d
Jarrow	14s 1d	14s 5d
Middlesborough	15s 1d	14s 5d
Newcastle	15s 1d	14s 7d
South Shields	14s 11d	14s 4d
Stockton	15s 2d	14s 7d
Sunderland	15s 0d	14s 8d [43]

The quality of life for the Belfast industrial worker was generally good. James Connolly, although he said many harsh things about Belfast, was forced to admit it offered definite advantages for the workforce:

> From the municipal point of view Belfast is a distinct improvement upon Dublin. Municipally, it can compare favourably with many similar cities in Great Britain, and its industrial conditions are the product of modern industrial slavery and can be paralleled wherever capitalism flourishes. The things in which Belfast is peculiar are the skilled use by the master class of religious rallying cries which, long since forgotten elsewhere, are still potent to limit and weaken labour here, and the pharisaical spirit of self-righteousness which enables unscrupulous sweaters of the poor, with one hand in the pocket of the workers, to raise the other to heaven and thank god that they are not as other men.
>
> When therefore, we say that Belfast is an improvement on Dublin from a municipal point of view we mean just exactly what we say, and nothing more, and would protest against more being read into our statement. The houses of the poor are better, house rent is lower, and the city is cleaner and healthier than Dublin.[44]

There was, however, an additional advantage enjoyed by Belfast over her rivals, which only becomes clear when the employment pattern of each centre is examined in detail. By 1901, 47% of Belfast's total population was listed by the census as being employed, 63% of males and 33% of females. Women formed 38% of the total labour force and, because of the importance of the linen industry, comprised an even higher proportion in manufacturing. This female employment was a critical difference when compared with other shipbuilding centres.

For Belfast's skilled working class, income could be greatly increased by the earnings of female members of the family who would perhaps have failed to find employment in other industrial centres. Even if wives did not normally work the availability of employment for women in periods of recession in the shipbuilding industry would have been a useful 'safety-net' for many families.

Once established, this elite became self-perpetuating, as did similar skilled groups in other industries and locations. Those who obtained apprenticeships in the shipyards were generally the sons of skilled workers. Compared to the Clyde, Belfast apprentice wages were lower and apprenticeship periods often longer. A skilled working class

family could support a boy through an apprenticeship as an investment for the future, but unskilled families lacked the resources to do
so.

FIGURE 12
Male/Female Employment in Shipbuilding Areas (1905)

	MANUFACTURING LABOUR FORCE	% MALE	% FEMALE
Belfast	100,890	56.6	43.7
Barrow	17,787	85.9	14.1
Birkenhead	22,926	69.2	30.8
Glasgow	203,752	69.0	31.0
Greenock	19,390	78.4	21.6
Jarrow	9,159	86.7	13.3
Middlesborough	20,376	88.4	11.6
Newcastle	49,435	77.3	22.7
South Shields	22,974	84.3	15.7
Stockton on Tees	12,039	89.9	16.1
Sunderland	31,547	80.3	19.7 [45]

Skilled labour was in short supply in Belfast and in consequence
such workers could demand high wages and reasonable employment
conditions in the yards. By contrast, unskilled labour was plentiful
and thus these workers were comparatively badly paid and badly
treated. There were enormous divisions between skilled and unskilled
workers in the Belfast shipyards. Again, this was certainly not unique
to either the industry or the area; similar antagonisms were a feature
of all contemporary British industries although political and religious
factors exacerbated these divisions in many cases. There were, as in all
industrial towns at this time, differences in the comparative standard
of living, as regards the quality of housing, quantity of food, social
activities and such like available to the skilled and unskilled. In
Belfast, however, there may have been a bitterness in these divisions
which was seldom found elsewhere, as the skilled elite was often dis-
tinguished from the unskilled by religion and background.

NOTES

1 Pollard and Robertson, *Shipbuilding*, p. 59.
2 Ibid., p. 56.
3 Moss and Hume, *Shipbuilders*.
4 Ibid., pp. 107–8.
5 Lynch, *Three cities*, pp. 94, 126–7.
6 Moss and Hume, *Shipbuilders*, pp., 162–3.
7 Ibid., pp. 510–19.
8 Ibid., p. 43.
9 Workman Clark, *Shipbuilding*, 'Particulars'.
10 *Belfast Trades Directory* (1896), Introduction.
11 Harland and Wolff Papers, PRONI D2805.
    There are numerous examples of which the following illustrate the point:
    • 28 March 1911 – Note of a telephone conversation concerning plans to increase wages of unskilled workers
    • 2 December 1911 – Letter from WC undertaking not to employ any striking H&W workers
    • 10 May 1913 – Letter to WC giving details of revised apprentice pay rates agreed by H&W
    • 1 April 1914 – Letter to WC containing list of striking boilermakers with request that they not be employed
12 Workman Clark, *Shipbuilding*, 'Particulars'.
13 Moss and Hume, *Shipbuilders*, pp. 510–19; Workman Clark, *Shipbuilding* 'Particulars'.
14 Workman Clark, *Shipbuilding*, 'Particulars'.
15 Ibid.
16 Ibid.
17 Lynch, 'Third Shipyard'.
18 *Belfast Trades Directory*, 1868, 1884, 1887, 1890, 1892.
19 Owen, *Belfast*, p. 304; Moss and Hume, *Shipbuilders*, p. 50.
20 Lynch, 'Third Shipyard', pp. 23–4.
21 BPP, Census of Ireland 1881, City of Belfast, table E.
22 Owen, *Belfast*, pp. 304–5; Coe, *Engineering*, p. 84.
23 Ibid.
24 *Industries of Ireland*, vol. 1, p. 72.
25 *Belfast Trades Directory*, 1887, 1890, 1892, Introduction.
26 *Lloyd's List*, 1884, 1890, 1895, 1898.
27 *Belfast Trades Directory*, 1894, Introduction.
28 Coe, *Engineering*, p. 84.
29 *Lloyd's Register*, 1895, 1897.
30 Kennedy and Ollerenshaw, *Economic history*, pp. 74–9.
31 Curtis, *Apes and angels*.
32 Budge and O'Leary, *Belfast*, p. 89.
33 Pounder, *Belfast-built*, p. 55.
34 Budge and O'Leary, *Belfast*, p. 75; Coe, *Engineering*, pp. 173–5.
35 Pollard and Robertson, *Shipbuilding*, p. 55.
    Pollard and Robertson's figures appear to have been distorted by the low wages paid to unskilled labour in Belfast, which was in plentiful supply, unlike a number of other regions.

36 BPP, *Census of Ireland*, 1861, 1871, 1881, 1891, 1901, 1911.

37 BPP, *Royal Commission on Labour*, Questions 26, 520–7.

38 BPP, *Working class rents, housing and retail prices.*

39 BPP, *Working class rents, housing and retail prices*, 1908, pp. 62–69, 75–80, 239–44, 311–17, 318–25, 421–27, 436-39, 446–52, 531–37, 539–42, 546–70.

40 BPP, *Statistical Tables and Charts*, H.C., 1905, XCVII, p. 23.
  The diets used to calculate this table comprised the following basic commodities:

	NORTH OF ENGLAND	SCOTLAND
Bread and Flour	27.64 lbs	26.97lbs
Meat	6.01 lbs	5.38lbs
Bacon	1.47 lbs	0.77lbs
Milk	9.49 pts	15.76 pts
Cheese	0.66 lbs	0.77 lbs
Butter	2.24 lbs	1.87 lbs
Potatoes	14.66 lbs	17.16 lbs
Oatmeal/Rice	0.65 lbs	5.33lbs
Tea	0.53 lbs	0.54 lbs
Sugar	5.17 lbs	5.29 lbs

41 Ibid.

42 Ibid.

43 BPP, *Working class rents, housing and retail prices.*

44 Connolly, 'Belfast and its problems', *Collected works*, p. 226.

45 BPP, *Working class housing, rents and retail prices.*

All work and no play? The Harland and Wolff sports team c. 1910.

3

LABOUR FORCE AND
INDUSTRIAL RELATIONS

W HO WORKED IN THE SHIPYARDS ON THE LAGAN when they were at the height of their success and how good were relations with their employers? It is possible to divide the workforce of the yards into broad groups: skilled, apprentices, semi-skilled, unskilled and white collar. Each of these groups had quite distinctive characteristics and related to other workers in the yards in different ways.

SKILLED MANUAL WORKERS

British shipbuilding in the nineteenth and early twentieth centuries was heavily dependent upon highly trained skilled labour. Such workers tended to share social origins and the experience of apprenticeship. Of those trades for which apprenticeships are listed in the Harland and Wolff papers, there were at least twenty-three broad categories in the yard, together with a large number of craftsmen classified by the firm as 'leading hands'. This is probably an underestimate, as other authors suggest that up to ninety trades could be found in a shipyard.[1] In the small yard of the Dublin Dockyard Co., which employed only 700 workers, there were forty-three groups of skilled men, together with thirty-two categories of specialist assistants and semi-skilled workers.[2] As regards Harland and Wolff, such skilled workers formed 50–60% of the labour force between 1912 and 1921, with the exact composition varying in accordance with the type of work being undertaken.[3] The proportion of skilled labour employed by Workman Clark was probably similar.

As a group such workers were difficult if not impossible to replace, as they formed a largely self-perpetuating elite within the labour force owing to the fact that their sons tended to be those who entered 'trades'. Amongst the problems they faced was the potential erosion of their position by new technology or other groups of skilled workers. The result was constant inter-union rivalry and demarcation disputes, as John Beattie, a full-time official of the Blacksmiths' and Ironworkers' Society, found in the period immediately following the First World War. Not only did he attempt to sort out a dispute between engine-smiths and ship-smiths within his own union, he also had problems with the plumbers about which trade should handle hydraulic pipework on cranes and weld flange connections on ships' engines. Equally he faced problems with Harland and Wolff on the question of the introduction of the 'Air Oliver', a device for making bolts, and the training of apprentice smiths in acetylene welding.[4]

Although skilled shipyard workers formed an elite within the shipyard work force, their working conditions remained harsh and frequently dangerous. During 1912, in the shipyards of the Lagan, Clyde, Tyne and Wear, seventy workers were killed and 2,848 injured as a result of falls or being hit by falling objects.[5] To these figures can be added persons killed or injured by drowning, fire, explosions or traffic accidents in a dangerous and congested working environment. James Connolly was to describe graphically the human cost of the shipbuilding industry in Belfast:

Our shipyards offer up a daily sacrifice of life and limb on the altar of capitalism. The clang of the ambulance bell is one of the most familiar daily sounds on the streets between our shipyards and our hospitals. It has been computed that some seventeen lives were lost on the *Titanic* before she left the Lagan; a list of the maimed and hurt and those suffering from minor injuries, as a result of the accidents at any one of these big ships would read like a roster of the wounded after a battle upon the Indian frontier.[6]

In 1907, forty-eight foundry workers in every thousand were subject to injury and their average life expectancy was about fifty-nine years.[7] The average life expectancy of members of the Amalgamated Society of Engineers was only forty-eight years at the end of the 1880s.[8] In such trades, physical injury or disability was a common – and accepted – feature of working life:

It may be taken as a fact based upon experience, that artisans who are exposed to such loud noises as are made in hammering rivets suffer from deafness. Boilermakers and riveters become deaf at an early age, while their comrades engaged in other kinds of work in the shipyard do not suffer.[9]

FIGURE 13

Skilled Workers Employed in the Belfast Yard of Harland and Wolff
Week Ending 27 August 1919[10]

	CRAFTSMEN	APPRENTICES
Joiners	2,144	89
Fitters	1,334	304
Riveters	703	376
Painters	525	16
Platers	472	116
Ironmoulders	446	54
Drillers	342	81
Shipwrights	317	130
Electricians	258	78
Turners	251	146
Plumbers	243	138
Smiths and Finishers	228	33
Caulkers	202	94
Patternmakers	123	38
Polishers	115	6

Sheet Metal Workers	87	44
Brass Founders	60	9
Upholsterers	51	5
Coppersmiths	46	21
Sawyers	43	4
Boatbuilders	9	0
Sailmakers	8	2

APPRENTICES

This group is related to and can be considered part of the skilled working class, as the majority of tradesmen learned their craft by this means. As previously mentioned, the major source of recruits for apprentices was the sons of skilled workers. An apprenticeship began at the age of sixteen and in most cases lasted for five years, although carpenters, joiners and painters served six and plumbers seven in the Belfast yards before the First World War.[11] Compared to the Clyde region, where opportunities for training were more plentiful, apprenticeships often lasted longer and rates of pay were usually lower. Parents had to pay a deposit of between two and five pounds against their son's good behaviour, a practice abandoned on the Clyde.[12] In addition, they had to meet the cost of the boy's tools, which could be a considerable outlay. A shipwright's tool kit lost in transit in 1915 was valued by its owner at £6 11s 4d, the equivalent of almost three weeks' pay at this time.[13]

Apprentices formed an important element of the labour force of the Belfast shipyards. In August 1919, Harland and Wolff employed 1,784 such trainees, representing 8.9% of the total labour force (see Figure 13).[14] Their status was ill-defined. On one level they acquired an increasing degree of skill but on another they were legally bound to remain with their employers for a period fixed by their articles of apprenticeship. They could and indeed were expected to join the trade societies of their respective skills, but were treated very much as second-class members by the time-served craftsmen. The Electricians, for example, only permitted apprentices to enrol in a specialist section, full membership being reserved for those who had completed their training. Equally, the Boilermakers allowed apprentices to join the union for benefit reasons but did not grant them full membership rights.[15] There were occasional revolts against such conditions in the Belfast shipyards, notably a major strike in 1913, which affected 1,300 apprentices in both yards.[16]

SEMI-SKILLED WORKERS

Pollard and Robertson, in their history of the British shipbuilding industry, suggest that 60-65% of the labour force in a British shipyard prior to the First World War was composed of skilled workers.[17] Harland and Wolff, from the limited detailed information available, employed a considerably lower proportion of skilled men, with only 49-60% of the labour force being skilled men or apprentices.[18] Pollard and Robertson have perhaps counted a number of groups of semi-skilled workers as skilled. In a letter to the City Clerk of Belfast, Harland and Wolff indicated that such groups as stagers, crane drivers, iron dressers, temporary lightmen and machinemen were regarded as semi-skilled.[19] The main difference between these men and the skilled worker is the fact that they did not undertake a formal apprenticeship, but rather 'picked up' the job by learning as they went along. According to the August 1919 list of 'hands employed', there were 2,122 semi-skilled workers of various categories employed in the yard, 10.6% of the work force.[20] In the Boilershop, where the figures available are less detailed, iron and brass dressers and machinemen formed 14.6% of the labour force.[21] It is probably fair to say that this group formed about one in eight of the total labour force in the Belfast shipyards and engine works.

It is difficult to judge the status of such workers compared to the 'skilled' groups. Although not the social equal of the skilled, the semiskilled performed a range of tasks which were critical to the shipbuilding process. One far from perfect indicator is perhaps wages. By late 1918 a semi-skilled rigger was paid almost as much as a sailmaker, a declining skilled trade. In contrast, he would have earned 8.5% less than a fitter, 11.5% less than a shipwright and 13% less than a patternmaker, although the gap had closed over the war years (see Figure 14).[22] Stagers, another semi-skilled group, were clearly less valued and earned only 54.4% of a patternmaker's weekly wage in early 1913.[23] It is difficult to compare rates of pay between Harland and Wolff and Workman Clark as the data are not available, although details of pay rates for stagers suggest they were not always identical.

FIGURE 14

Wages of Stagers in Belfast Shipyards 1899–1913[24]

	DATE AWARDED	
	HARLAND AND WOLFF	WORKMAN CLARK
19s	before March 1899	September 1905
19s 6d	March 1899	
20s	March 1911	June 1910
21s	January 1912	August 1911
22s	August 1912	August 1912
24s	January 1913	February 1913

The intermediate nature of semi-skilled workers can be seen clearly by examining their trade union affiliations. A number of groups were readily admitted by craft unions. For example, the Boilermakers recruited 'holders up' and the Electricians organised temporary light men.[25] Other groups formed local bodies such as the Belfast Ship Riggers' Protective Society, although there was a tendency for such bodies to amalgamate into larger national societies or be absorbed by craft unions.[26] A number of groups within the shipyards joined labourers' unions like the crane drivers and iron dressers in Harland and Wolff's boilershop, who were members of the National Amalgamated Union of Labour (NAUL) by 1911.[27]

THE UNSKILLED

In 1911, Samuel Bartlett of Harland and Wolff's pay office reported that the firm employed 589 'labourers, watchmen and storemen', together with 1,139 unskilled workers in the shipyard and 1,596 in the engine works.[28] By 1919, Harland and Wolff employed 7,423 unskilled workers in the shipyard, including 641 boys, 37.0% of the labour force.[29] The Engine shop is more difficult to assess, owing to the way in which figures were compiled; however, it seems likely that the proportion of unskilled here was higher than in the shipyards, with up to 50% of the labour force being in this category. These workers were a largely casual group, with few skills which could not easily be replaced. Unlike a number of other shipbuilding regions, Belfast had a surplus of unskilled labour. As a result, wages for this group, in contrast to skilled labour which was scarce, were amongst

A rather staged photograph of workers assembling a turbine casing for
the *Britannic*. The scene shows well the social division within the labour force,
the ordinary workers in their overalls and flat caps being supervised by
a foreman in suit and bowler.

the lowest in the United Kingdom.

However, the division between the skilled and unskilled in Belfast's
shipyards was not merely one of pay, but also of status. The ill-feeling
between the groups was clearly demonstrated in a series of interviews
conducted in 1959 by Sam Hanna Bell, for a radio programme on the
1907 Belfast Dock Strike.[30] Bob Getgood, the Belfast organiser of the
Workers' Union, had very clear memories of relations between the
two groups:

> There was no association. The labourers herded off together, went off
> together. But an odd one would have curried favour with a foreman
> but was more likely to be currying favour with his skilled employee.
> He was anxious to be on good terms with him because his job was
> more secure. He felt that if he could be on good terms with the
> craftsman then his value to the craftsman was seen and if a choice had

to be made he was more likely to be retained in preference to the fellow who was, probably a better man but harder to work with.[31]

In another of these interviews, William Hunter, who had worked as a carter during the strike, saw the differences between the skilled and unskilled as social in origin:

> The craftsman he had something the other unfortunate soul didn't have. Now that came about due to the fact that the parents could afford to put their child to a trade. They were all humans – they were equal in every other way – but their parents could not afford to give them a trade. Perhaps they had as good an education but the indentures and the one thing and another that had to be laid down for to get a trade many families could not afford.[32]

William Hughes, also a carter, recalled that the skilled workers disapproved of the unskilled joining unions. However, he recollected that, in some circumstances, the situation was reversed – then, the dockers and carters would not permit skilled men to obtain casual work on the docks if employment was slack in the yards.[33]

The main union that represented unskilled and semi-skilled workers in the Belfast shipyards was the National Amalgamated Union of Labour (NAUL), established in the Tyneside shipyards amongst platers' helpers and others directly employed by craftsmen of the Boilermakers' Union.[34] The *raison d'être* of the new body on Tyneside was to protect the helpers from exploitation by skilled workers, rather than from confrontation with the yard owners. The Belfast yards also experienced similar tensions within their labour force. In March 1889 a strike occurred involving two hundred platers' helpers and rivet heaters against, contemporaries noted, the skilled platers under whom they worked rather than the shipyard owners.[35] The craft unions were very slow and begrudging in accepting the unionisation of unskilled workers in the yards. The NAUL was not admitted to the Federation of Engineering and Shipbuilding Trades until 1908 and the National Union of Gasworkers and General Labourers were not permitted to join until 1910. Even then, both unions had to 'know their place' and the refusal of another important union representing unskilled shipyard labour, the Worker's Union, to 'give assurances' to the Engineers resulted in their exclusion.[36] The NAUL was not included in the Articles of Agreement between Harland and Wolff and the unions because, unlike the skilled craftsmen, their members were replaceable.

It would be wrong to present the relations between Belfast's ship-builders and the unskilled labour in their yards as entirely hostile, par-ticularly in the case of Harland and Wolff. The NAUL, for example, had been able to organise a large sector of the yard's labour and had therefore to be treated with respect. In 1911, for example, the union wrote to the management enclosing a copy of a resolution passed by their members in the foundry department:

> After the 4th of October, we, the individual members of the National Amalgamated Union of Labour, employed as labourers, iron dressers, cranemen etc. employed in Messrs Harland and Wolff's foundry department, will cease to work with any person employed in said department who is eligible to become a member but who on the aforesaid date has not joined the National Amalgamated Union of Labour.[37]

The reply of the company to this uncompromising demand for the imposition of a closed shop amongst unskilled and semi-skilled work-ers was both moderate and conciliatory in tone:

> As you are aware, the firm have always fully recognised the various trade and labour unions, and have endeavoured to work amicably with them, and we are somewhat surprised that your members should take this step. We hope, however, that on further considera-tion they will see some other way out of the difficulty.[38]

The relationship was reasonably positive and both sides extended co-operation, as can be seen in June 1913, when the company wrote to the union:

> We regret having to complain of the bad time keeping of the platers' helpers and angle iron smiths' helpers. From one fourth to one third of the platers' helpers are absent every morning and quite a number absent every day. The angle iron smiths' helpers are even worse. We would be glad if you can do anything to effect an improvement.[39]

The union's reply, whilst expressing relief that the smiths' helpers who were represented by a rival union had a worse record than their members, was not in any way antagonistic or defensive. It enclosed a copy of a notice which it had sent to every platers' helper in the yard:

> For some time past the firm has strongly complained about bad time

keeping on the part of a large section of our helper members. So bad has this become lately that they have decided to take drastic action to deal with this evil unless there is a marked change in the immediate future. No union can defend bad time keeping and we therefore hope this warning will have the desired effect.

WHITE COLLAR WORKERS

Harland and Wolff's 'office' in late 1919 contained about 5% of the total work force, if timekeepers, pay office staff, workers in the drawing office, foremen, messengers and porters are included.[40] These workers, who came primarily from the middle and upper working classes, were in many cases highly trained and experienced supervisors and technicians. It was considered a 'step up' if an apprentice, on completion of training, was taken 'upstairs' into the office. Certainly in terms of status, the office staff considered themselves above those in the yard and works. The comparative status of the various groups of office workers can be seen in their rates of pay. A draughtsman, for example, earned between £5 3s and £5 9s by August 1919, depending on the department in which he worked.[41] In 1921 clerks, who were expected to serve a five year apprenticeship, received an average of £4 2s 2d a week.[42] In August 1918, the average wage of ninety-five timekeepers employed by the firm was £3 7s per week.[43]

There was a definite hierarchy within the shipyard 'office', with the topmost layer being formed by the 'managers' who actually ran the yard. In 1919, Harland and Wolff employed fifty-four individuals at this level. Below these came the supervisory grades. Harland's employed 136 head and assistant foremen and storekeepers, highly experienced and valued individuals who effectively ran the yard on a day-to-day basis. At the same time, the firm employed 330 workers in the drawing office and 161 timekeepers and piecework counters in the pay office. Clerical support, including typists, was provided by 453 workers, a modest 1.6% of the total labour force. To this small organisation was added twenty staff working in the dining room, six hall porters and 101 messengers and porters.[44]

As a group, office workers in the shipyards were slow to unionise, as comparatively good conditions combined with vulnerability to victimisation, made union membership less attractive to them than it was for other groups. However, during the First World War a certain amount of progress was made. By late 1918, Harland and Wolff had begun to discuss war bonus payments with the National Union of Clerks and meetings were held with that body after the war.[45] In 1920 the union appointed a full-time official in Belfast, where 'there was a substantial membership in the shipbuilding industry'.[46] The Association of Shipbuilding and Engineering Draughtsmen was active in Belfast from late 1916 and, by the following year, was strong enough to justify the attendance of two delegates to national meetings rather than the one which most other branches sent.[47] Various trade unions were formed to represent foremen and other supervisory staff during the war years, but none was ever recognised by the Shipbuilders' Federation.[48] In addition, there appears to have been a local society representing such staff in Harland and Wolff, which took the form of the Foremans' Mutual Aid and Social Society. A letter to the management during the 1919 strike, however, would indicate that the latter was not a particularly militant body:

> I am instructed by a number of foremen and assistants in your employ to inform you that they were turned back by pickets on the Queen's Road this morning and informed that this was the only warning they would receive and if they persisted on going, it would be at their own risk. Hoping this will be a satisfactory explanation of our absence from work.[49]

WOMEN

A final group of workers in the Belfast yards – women – are frequently forgotten. Although employment in the industry was predominantly male, it was by no means exclusively so. As conscription was never introduced into Ireland there was no need to recruit female labour on the scale seen in a number of other regions during the First World War. However, a report dated July 1916 records that there were 151 women working in the yard, that is 1.7% of the labour force. No details were given as to their employment. It seems likely that they were unskilled cleaners or workers from skilled groups such as upholsterers or French polishers, which contained a high proportion of women. The only groups for which details were given were waitresses (nineteen) and charwomen (twenty-two), who were employed in the 'office' rather than the yard.[50]

By 1919 the main area of female employment was the 'office'. Included here would have been tracers in the drawing office, typists (a group increasingly but by no means exclusively female) and clerical workers. Moss and Hume note that the last workers to suffer as a result of the expulsions in 1920 were female – four waitresses in Harland and Wolff's staff dining room who were driven out on 27 August 1920 [51] (see p. 57).

INDUSTRIAL RELATIONS

One of the major claims made by Moss and Hume in their history of Harland and Wolff concerns industrial relations within the firm during the two decades before the First World War:

> The Company's industrial relations had been remarkably good since the 1895 strike. There had only been a handful of trivial disputes since the formation of the committee of managing directors in 1907.[52]

They also suggest that the firm enjoyed excellent relations with the unions and indeed on occasion acted as an arbitrator in demarcation disputes between different groups of skilled men. This certainly makes the firm appear decidedly liberal and advanced when compared to certain other companies in the British shipbuilding industry. However, there are factors which undermine this image of paternalistic harmony. In the years before the First World War, the desire to maintain good relations with the unions applied mainly to those representing skilled men. It is notable that Harland and Wolff did not include those unions representing unskilled workers in the Memorandum of Agreement of July 1914 (this was basically an agreement between Harland and Wolff and the unions representing skilled workers to refer demarcation and other disputes to arbitration rather than striking. Although primarily intended to safeguard production the agreement was fairly advanced in terms of labour relations).[53] The main objective of this agreement was to establish a structure for settling demarcation disputes between trades, a problem not encountered amongst the unskilled.

Moss and Hume mention only two serious labour disputes prior to 1895: in 1884 on the question of wage reductions and in 1886 on the political issue of Home Rule.[54] This appears a very creditable record, but is it complete? There was certainly a month-long stoppage which affected the shipyards in 1887, in protest against the introduction of fortnightly pay amongst engineers and boilermakers.[55] The history of the Boilermakers' Society also mentions a dispute in Belfast involving over 5,000 workers in 1888, which must have affected the shipyards. This is confirmed by the Board of Trade reports.[56] In fact, the Reports of the Board of Trade into Strikes and Lockouts records at least seventeen industrial disputes in Belfast which affected the shipbuilding industry between 1888 and 1894. It would appear, therefore, that Moss and Hume's statement that the dispute of 1895 'seems to have been the first major industrial dispute in the firm's history' is questionable.[57]

What were the industrial problems faced by Belfast's shipbuilders? The 1895 dispute indicates that industrial relations between employer and labour force were not as harmonious as the company history would have us believe. The origin of the strike lay in a carefully planned attempt by the employers on the Lagan and Clyde to introduce joint bargaining procedures in both centres.[58] When the Belfast yards struck in protest, the Scottish employers began to lay off workers at a rate of 25% per week, in an attempt to coerce the unions.[59] Although Moss and Hume suggest that the strike in Belfast collapsed in the face of determined management action, the unions' version of events suggests that the strikers were not in a mood to compromise:

> The first offer made by the employers was rejected by both Belfast and the Clyde men, but in January 1896, a further offer which constituted a partial victory for the unions was accepted by the latter but not the former. The Clyde strikers outnumbered the Belfast men by more than two to one, with the result that the majority of the aggregate votes were in favour of the settlement and the Executive Council ordered the Belfast men to return to work along with the Clyde members and they considered their strength had been dissipated by the extension of the dispute and did not feel bound by the result of the joint vote. 'Betrayal' was only one word used in Belfast, and the feeling against the Executive ran high. To enforce their decision, the Executive had to suspend the payment of all contingent benefits there.[60]

Such bitterness and determination would seem to indicate that relationships between the Belfast shipbuilders and their employees were anything but harmonious.

Fitters in the engine shop of Harland and Wolff installing turbine blades with sledgehammers! The number 433 indicates that this unit was destined for the White Star liner *Britannic*, launched in 1914.

Another claim by Moss and Hume is that Harland and Wolff and Workman Clark remained aloof from the Shipbuilders' Employers' Federation, a body which at times was bitterly opposed to trade unionism.[61] This may have been true in so far as neither firm paid a membership fee, but in the Harland and Wolff papers there are several files of correspondence with employers' organisations. Furthermore, the relationship went beyond the exchange of information:

WILLIAM GALLOCHER: RIVETER

Messrs Napier and Miller Ltd, one of the members of this association, advise that the above named riveter started a berth on the shell of a vessel at present being built in their yard, and left the same without completing his job. He is understood to have found employment in Belfast.

I shall be obliged by your kindly giving the usual co-operation.[62]

STRIKE OF SHIPWRIGHTS: BELFAST

Messrs Harland and Wolff Ltd, Belfast, advise that their shipwrights struck on Wednesday last on a question of a demarcation of work between themselves and the joiners. They went out without giving notice, and the firm ask that the members of the Federation might be advised of the stoppage. In some cases the Belfast firms have been asked by the Federation for co-operation in similar circumstances.

Please advise your members of the foregoing, and invite their co-operation when setting on shipwrights during the current strike in Belfast.[63]

The Belfast employers may not have been members of the employers' federation but, given this level of co-operation, they can hardly be said to have opposed the ideals of such a body.

On balance, the Belfast shipyards were probably reasonably good employers. Having said that, they had little real choice as they needed to retain scarce labour and maintain production in a highly competitive market. After 1895, the Belfast shipbuilders did not join in co-ordinated efforts to reduce or break union power within their work forces but, rather, tried to maintain reasonable working relations. However, despite this somewhat self-interested liberalism, there were a large number of industrial disputes in the Belfast yards, many of which cannot be described as 'trivial'. Although after 1901, only disputes recognised as 'major' were reported by the Board of Trade there were still eight outbreaks of industrial unrest in the city's shipyards worthy of mention before the outbreak of the First World War.[64]

Many of these disputes had nothing to do with employers but, rather, were the result of conflicts between groups of skilled workers or between skilled and unskilled labour within the yards. Demarcation disputes were a feature of the British shipbuilding industry in these years. Although now they may seem petty and pointless, it should be remembered that the main reason for such action was to safeguard the employment of groups of skilled workers within a rapidly changing industry. As some trades declined in importance they were forced to fight to retain employment in the yards, whilst others aggressively tried to create monopolies. A classic example of this process were the shipwrights, workers who had been the primary trade in shipbuilding yards in the days of wood, but who initially refused to adapt to working in iron. In 1850, 90% of new tonnage had been built in wood; by 1880 this had fallen to only 4%.[65] Within a generation, therefore, these workers had declined from being the principal shipbuilding trade to a point where they desperately tried to prevent encroachment by carpenters on what was left of their work. This friction between shipwrights and carpenters was a major problem in Belfast, as John MacIlwaine informed the Royal Commission on Labour in 1893.[66] Demarcation disputes between the two trades led to strikes in Belfast in 1890, 1891, 1911 and 1913, with the shipwrights in every case losing work to the carpenters.[67]

Another frequent source of inter-union conflict occurred when competing unions represented the same group of tradesmen. In 1892, Belfast saw an astonishing example of this, in the rivalry between the United Kingdom Pattern Makers Association (UKPA) and the Amalgamated Society of Engineers (ASE). UKPA planned strike action and appealed to the ASE, who also recruited patternmakers, to support the action or at least undertake not to break it. This was agreed only after a direct appeal from the General Secretary of UKPA.[68] After a few days of strike action, ASE circulated employers, offering to supply patternmakers, with the result that the industrial action collapsed and a number of UKPA members lost their jobs.[69] The National Executive of the ASE assumed full responsibility for this action, claiming that UKPA members had stated that they would not end their strike until ASE members who remained at work were dismissed. The UKPA denied that such a demand had been made and a furious row ensued. It is difficult to say which party was in the wrong but the history of the UKPA offers a plausible explanation:

> It was quite clear that one of our members never made such a threat, although it might have been true that some individual, probably in his cups, said something which aroused the indignation of someone else, probably in a similar condition.[70]

The problem of aggressive trade unionism is well illustrated by the difficulties faced by the Tin Plate Workers' Union (TPWU) in the shipyards. At the end of the nineteenth century this body was under pressure from the much more powerful Boilermakers' Society, which began recruiting light plate workers with a view to claiming all such work in the yards. In 1898, this confrontation was resolved by the TPWU agreeing to surrender to the Boilermakers all work involving sheet metal over one-eighth of an inch thick.[71] However, no sooner was this done than the Glasgow Branch of the TPWU seceded and formed the Sheet Iron and Light Platers' Society in 1900. Although initially consisting of only sixty-eight members, the new union began an aggressive policy of membership poaching aimed at driving their former colleagues out of the yards.[72] In the north-east yards of the Tyne, Tees and Wear, relations deteriorated to the point where the Federation of Engineering and Shipbuilding Trades initiated an enquiry, which publicly rebuked the Light Platers' methods as 'wanting in the spirit of fair play and recognised trade union principles'.[73] This did nothing to cause the Light Platers to change their policy or methods and the two unions remained bitter rivals. Both bodies were present in Harland and Wolff and signed the Memorandum of Agreement in 1914.

Not all unions indulged in such fratricidal conflicts and, again, Harland and Wolff offers an example of co-operation. Amongst the eighteen bodies, which signed the Memorandum of Agreement in July 1914, was the Amalgamated and General Society of Carpenters.[74] There is something of a mystery in this, as no such union is known to have existed. Rather this appears to have been a joint committee representing the General Union of Carpenters and Joiners and the Amalgamated Society of Carpenters and Joiners. Both bodies were independent; indeed, the General Union rejected amalgamation with the newer and larger body in 1902, 1904 and 1907. The two societies were not to combine until 1921, when they formed the Amalgamated Society of Woodworkers.[75] The joint committee, however, was clearly more than a temporary negotiating body for, as early as April 1911, it had written to the company concerning the employment of non-union carpenters.[76] Whatever the feelings at national level, the carpenters in Harland's were capable of working together to protect their own interests.

Relations between skilled and unskilled labour in the Belfast ship-yards were also fraught at times. Following an initial strike by platers' helpers against the conditions being imposed upon them by skilled team leaders in March 1889, there were at least five other strikes of a similar nature.[77] In 1893, a strike was provoked by the platers attempting to pass on to their teams a 5% wage reduction, which they had agreed with Harland and Wolff. In order to get production restarted, the company therefore agreed to pay the difference in wages.[78] A strike in 1897 saw a strange inversion of the 'normal' situation, when a shop steward of the NAUL was sacked and a four-day strike resulted in his reinstatement. However, the platers refused to work whilst the shop steward was employed and the impasse was only broken by his resignation.[79]

The unions representing the unskilled may have enjoyed reasonable relations with their employers in the shipyards but their relations with the skilled unions were less than fraternal. In an interview in 1959, Bob Getgood spoke of conditions for the unskilled in the yards around the time of the First World War:

> And there was his craft pride – I must give him credit for his craft pride. But he hadn't the broad human touch of the other fellow who carried the mud to him, carried the mortar to him, carried the machine – so I found in the shipyard – got into the hole and with the seat of his pants cleaned that part of the boat and got threepence for cleaning it. And when the skilled man went after it was cleaned he got a shilling for working in a dirty corner.[80]

In view of such conditions, it is hardly surprising that the NAUL and other unions representing unskilled workers found the shipyards a fruitful recruiting ground.

NOTES

1 Pollard and Robertson, *British Shipbuilding*, p. 154.
2 Smellie, *Ship building and repairing*, pp. 150, 63-5.
3 Harland and Wolff Papers, 25/7/1912, 10/3/1915, 27/8/1919, 20/7/1920, 20/6/1921.
4 Tuckett, *Blacksmiths' history*, p. 212.
5 BPP, *Accidents in shipbuilding yards*, p. 3.
6 Connolly, 'Belfast and its Problems', vol. 1, p. 233.
7 Fyrth and Collins, *The foundry workers*, pp. 114-5.
8 Jefferys, *Story of the Engineers*, pp. 76-7.
9 Oliver, *Dangerous trades*, p. 752.
10 Harland and Wolff Papers, 27/8/1919.
11 Harland and Wolff Papers, 27/8/1912, letter to Govan Shipyard.
12 Ibid.
13 Ibid., early 1915.
14 Ibid., 27/8/1918.
15 Stevens, *Story of E.T.U.*, p. 60; Mortimer, *Boilermakers' Society*, vol. 1, p. 122.
16 BPP, *Board of Trade Strikes and Lockouts*, 1913.
17 Pollard and Robertson, *Shipbuilding*, p. 153.
18 Harland and Wolff Papers, 25/7/1912, 10/3/1915, 27/8/1919, 20/7/1920, 20/6/1921.
19 Ibid., 19/4/1920.
20 Ibid., 19/4/1920: Cranemen, Smiths Strikers, Firemen, Stagers, Iron Dressers, Donkey Boilermen, Temporary Lightmen, Drillers*.
   27/8/1919: Holders up, Brass Dressers, Upholsters Stitchers, Brass Finishers, Riggers, Boltmakers, Screwers.
   *Although there is reference to Drillers as being semi-skilled they appear as apprentices and therefore I have counted them as skilled. This perhaps represents a distinction between hand-drillers and machine-drillers.
21 Ibid., 28/6/1919.
22 Ibid., September 1919.
23 Ibid., 28/2/1919.
24 Ibid., 28/2/1913.
25 Stevens, *Story of E.T.U.*, p. 60; Mortimer, *Boilermakers' Society*, p. 122.
26 Ward-Perkins, *Trade union records*, p. 241.
27 Harland and Wolff Papers, 2/12/1911.
28 Ibid., 15/3/1911.

GENERAL	SHIPYARD		ENGINESHOP	
Labourers	Scrapers	363	Boilermakers' Helpers	636
Watchmen	Fitters' Assistants	202	Fitters' Assistants	739
Sweepers	Plumbers' Assistants	238	Coppersmiths' Assistants	76
Storemen	Carters' Assistants	15	Labourers	116
	Sailmakers' Assistants	4	Wood Labourers	29
	Electrical Labourers	111		
TOTAL		933		1596

29 Ibid., 27/8/1919.
30 PRONI, Hanna Bell Papers, D3358/1.
31 Ibid., interview with Bob Getgood.
32 Ibid., interview with William Hunter.

33 Ibid., interview with William Hughes.
34 Clegg, Fox and Thompson, *British trade unions*, p. 66.
35 BPP, *Board of Trade Strikes and Lockouts*, 1889.
36 Coates and Topham, *Transport and General Workers Union*, p. 513.
37 Harland and Wolff Papers, 2/12/1911.
38 Ibid., 3/12/1911.
39 Ibid., 21/6/1913.
40 Ibid., 22/12/1919.
41 Ibid., 18/8/1919.
42 Ibid., 18/8/1921.
43 Ibid., letter to NUC late 1918.
44 Ibid., 22/12/1919.
45 Ibid., undated, late 1918, 15/10/1921.
46 Hughes, *Hand and brain*, p. 64.
47 Mortimer, *Draughtsmen*, pp. 28, 39.
48 Marsh and Ryan, *Directory of Trade Unions*, Amalgamated Managers' and
   Foreman's' Society, pp. 4–5; National Foremans' Association, pp. 40–1;
   Association of Supervisory Staffs, Executives and Technicians, p. 151.
49 Harland and Wolff Papers, 28/1/1919.
50 Ibid., 31/7/1916.
51 Moss and Hume, *Shipbuilders*, p. 225.
52 Ibid., p. 168.
53 Ibid., pp. 170–7.
54 Ibid., pp. 49, 55.
55 Patterson, *Class conflict and sectarianism*, p. 26.
56 Mortimer, *Boilermakers' Society*, vol. 1, p. 112; BPP. *Board of Trade Strikes and
   Lockouts*, 1888.
57 Moss and Hume, *Shipbuilders*, p. 75.
58 Dougan, *Shipwrights*, p. 94.
59 Moss and Hume, *Shipbuilders*, pp. 74–5.
60 Jefferys, *Engineers*, p. 141.
61 Moss and Hume, *Shipbuilders*, pp. 89-90, 170, 284-5.
62 Harland and Wolff Papers, 29/9/1911.
63 Ibid.
64 BPP, *Board of Trade Strikes and Lockouts*, 1901.
   After this report only disputes involving 300 workers or more or lasting more
   than 15,000 man/days were classified as 'major' and included in the report.
   August 1911: Rivet Heaters, 241 strikers and 331 affected; *November–December
   1911*: Joiners (H&W) demarcation dispute, 700 strikers; *August 1912*:
   Unskilled Workers both yards, 700 strikers; *January–February 1913*:
   Apprentices both yards, 1,300 strikers; *February 1913*: Apprentices,
   300 strikers; *April 1913*: Platers, 300 strikers, 300 affected; *May–June 1913*:
   Joiners, 540 strikers; *August–September 1913*: Shipwrights, H&W, 362 strikers.
65 Jefferys, *Engineers*, p. 45.
66 BPP, *Royal Commission on Labour*.
67 BPP, *Board of Trade Strikes and Lockouts*, 1890,1891,1911, 1913.
68 Mosses, *Pattern Makers*, pp. 99–100.
69 BPP, *Board of Trade Strikes and Lockouts*, 1892.
70 Mosses, *Pattern Makers*, pp. 99–100.
71 Kidd, *Tin-plate workers*, p. 169.
72 Marsh and Ryan, *Historical Directory*, vol. 2, pp. 122–3.
73 Kidd, *Tin-plate workers*, p. 179.

[74] Moss and Hume, *Shipbuilders*, pp. 170–2.
[75] Marsh and Ryan, *Historical Directory*, vol. 3, pp. 21–2, 24–5.
[76] Harland and Wolff Papers, April 1911.
[77] BPP, *Board of Trade Strikes and Lockouts*.
[78] Ibid., 1894.
[79] Ibid., 1897.
[80] Hanna Bell Papers, interview with Bob Getgood.

4

BOOM AND BUST
1914–1935

A S WITH MANY OTHER ASPECTS OF BRITISH SOCIETY, the years between 1914 and 1918 marked a turning point in the Belfast shipbuilding industry for these years saw the end of a golden era and the beginning of decline, although this was not recognised at the time. The Belfast shipyards had never built warships in any number, although both Harland and Wolff and Workman Clark had carried out a limited amount of work for the Admiralty.[1] The history of the two Belfast yards at this period followed a similar pattern and they can be discussed together. The outbreak of war found their slips full of merchant vessels; like all yards without Admiralty work on hand, they were thrown into chaos as material was diverted to urgent naval construction. The building lists of both yards show that vessels on the stocks were greatly delayed by such shortages and ships due for launching in 1914–15 were often not off the slips until 1916–17.

Although Workman Clark were to claim that 'the firm was occupied solely with Admiralty orders',[2] their production was limited to small warships and auxiliaries with output amounting to thirty-one boom defence vessels, sloops, patrol boats and stern wheel hospital ships for use on the rivers of Mesopotamia.[3] In addition, they built two small coastal monitors on a sub-contract basis for Harland and Wolff.[4] The warship output of Harland's consisted mainly of monitors of various classes, although a couple of major warships were also constructed, namely the cruiser *Cavendish* and the light battle-cruiser *Glorious*.[5] The *Glorious* of 22,354 tons was laid down in early 1915, launched in April 1916 and finally delivered in December of that year. Despite the fact that the ship represented one of the most misbegotten developments of the entire ill-conceived battle-cruiser concept which resulted in battleship sized vessels with cruiser armour, there is no denying that this was an impressive achievement for a yard with limited naval experience. The *Cavendish* was laid down on No. 2 slip as soon as the *Glorious* was launched and proved to be a less happy experience for Harland and Wolff. Originally the name ship of a class of powerful fleet cruisers, the design was changed in mid-1917, just before launching, and the ship was rebuilt as an aircraft carrier. The extensive alterations required to the almost completed hull delayed launching until January 1918, thus depriving the firm of one of its best-equipped slips at a critical time.[6]

From 1917 there was a major shift in British shipbuilding policy, for with the German submarine campaign now at its peak, losses in merchant shipping reached critical levels. Few merchant vessels had been laid down since 1914, so standardised merchant ships were placed at the top of construction priorities. Belfast, with its pre-war merchant shipping specialisation, inevitably played a significant part in such a programme; furthermore, the appointment of William Pirrie as Controller of Shipping with responsibility for the programme ensured that the Belfast yards were to be major contributors. The first 'Standard Merchant Ship', an 'A' type cargo vessel named

The effects of the war can clearly be seen in these two pictures of Workman Clark's north yard. In addition to modern cranes on most building slips three new slips were constructed, one of which was capable of accommodating a vessel of over 1,000 feet in length.

War Shamrock, was launched by Harland and Wolff in June 1917 and delivered in August. Soon the yard was producing little but standard ships. Another dozen were completed before the end of the war and a further twenty-three were at various stages of construction.[7] Workman Clark also began producing standard ships as soon as their slips were cleared, the first to be launched being *War Beetle* in 1918. Two others were completed by the end of the war, by which point a further twelve 'A' 'B' and 'G' types were also under construction.[8] The speed of construction was of critical importance, as Belfast City Council recorded at the end of the war:

> Some of these vessels have been turned out in very quick time. During their construction one of the firm's men [Workman Clark] established a new world's riveting record in the north yard, the south yard and engine works replying by making a record in the way of finishing a standard ship, an 8,000 ton vessel being completed in 3 3/4 days from the time of launch.[9]

Although construction of new vessels in Belfast was considerable, the main contribution of the Lagan yards to the allied war effort lay in other work. Throughout the war, the north of Ireland was seen as a secure area, difficult for U-boats to reach and thus safe from German attacks. For this reason, Belfast became a major repair and refit centre for naval and merchant vessels. The history of Workman Clark shows the scale of such work:

> during that period 1,396 vessels were handled either for building [only 77 vessels], repairing or overhauling ... the vessels dealt with approximated one for every day of the war.[10]

The first major task undertaken by Workman Clark was the conversion of four obsolete cruisers into coastal bombardment vessels for use off Flanders. This project was completed extremely rapidly by employing day and night shifts.[11] A merchant vessel was reconstructed and equipped with fitting shops, moulding shops, a foundry and various other machine shops before being commissioned as the destroyer depot ship *Sandhurst* capable, it was noted, of carrying out 'repairs of any reasonable kind'. This meant that vessels did not have to return to base dockyards.[12] Large numbers of liners were fitted out as hospital vessels or troop transports, whilst a number including *Coronado*, *Mantua*, *Patia* and *Patuca* were converted into auxiliary

A stern-wheel hospital ship, one of four flat-bottomed vessels completed by
Workman Clark in 1917 for use on the rivers of Mesopotamia.

cruisers.[13] All sections of the yard were fully employed:

> The engine works erected the boilers and engines in all the vessels
> built in the shipyard, and in addition carried out an enormous quan-
> tity of repair work and overhaul work to engines and boilers of
> almost every kind of craft in the Navy.[14]

The workload of Harland and Wolff appears to have been even
heavier. One of their strangest tasks involved the conversion of a
number of merchant ships into a dummy battle fleet to confuse
German intelligence in the early days of the war.[15] These ships were
subsequently returned to the yard for conversion into troop transports or supply vessels from early 1915.[16] In addition to this, a large
number of ships were converted to troop or hospital ships and a huge
amount of repair work was undertaken. The yard acted as the main
repair and maintenance base for the naval vessels of the Irish Sea
patrol squadrons.[17] It was perhaps this less glamorous work of repair
and refit, which represented Belfast's major contribution to the war at
sea between 1914 and 1918.

The yards were operating flat out to meet the demands of civilian
and military construction and repair work at this time and labour,
which was never plentiful, was increasingly in short supply. Despite a

definite policy by Harland and Wolff to retain skilled labour whenever possible, by 1915 the firm was reduced to poaching skilled workers from Workman Clark and local engineering firms.[18] Production and industrial harmony were only maintained by generous 'cost of living' allowances and the extensive use of overtime. In the week ending 27 April 1915, seventy-five workers in the yard worked over eighty hours and a further 1,164 employees worked between sixty and eighty.[19] Such working conditions could not be maintained indefinitely but the company could only recruit limited numbers of additional workers. Despite this, they tried to limit the dilution of skilled labour and refused to recruit large numbers of women, as occurred elsewhere in Britain.[20] As late as July 1916, a return shows that only 163 of the 13,429 workers employed in the shipyard were female.[21]

Wages increased at an unprecedented rate for shipyard workers (see Figure 15) and the demand for labour during the war and the short post-war boom was intense:

> After the war Arthur Pollock put the barbers shop up for sale, he was moving to the shipyard. That's how good the work was in those days in the shipyard. Men would leave a business to go and work in it. I took the shop over.[22]

Such wage increases were necessary to cover the massive increase in the cost of living in these years. The *Labour Gazette* of October 1922 was quoted by the Belfast branch of the Electrical Trades Union to show that there had been a 121% increase in prices during the war years.[23] To prove their point, they calculated that the weekly food ration of a third-class officer in the Belfast union – which had cost 6s 3d in July 1914 – cost 16s in October 1921.[24] In September 1919 the patternmakers at Harland and Wolff requested a pay rise partly to cover the increased cost of tools, which had doubled during the war years.[25]

Understandably, in view of the financial sacrifice involved and the need for skilled labour, most shipyard workers preferred to stay at home rather than enlist in the armed forces; as late as August 1917, there were 150 unemployed joiners seeking work in Belfast's yards.[27] Fr John Hassan writing under the pseudonym of G.B. Kenna was later to claim, in what was admittedly a very hostile account, that it was doubtful if 5% of the shipyards workers enlisted during the war.[28]

FIGURE 15

Wage Rates in Harland and Wolff's shipyard 1897–1918

	FITTER	PATTERNMAKER	SHIPWRIGHT	RIGGER	SAILMAKER
1897	36s	38s	37s 2d	30s	32s
1898	37s	39s	38s 3d	30s 6d	
1903	36s		37s 2d		
1906	37s				
1908		40s			
1911 a	38s	41s			
b	39s	42s	40s 6d	31s 6d	33s
1912	40s	43s		33s 6d	36s
1913	41s	44s			
1915 a	44s	47s	46s	38s 6d	39s
b	46s	49s	48s	40s 6d	41s
1916	49s	52s	51s	43s 6d	44s
1917 a	54s	57s	56s	48s 6d	49s
b	57s	60s	59s	51s 6d	52s
c	62	69s	64s	56s 6d	57s
1918 a	65s 6d	68s 6d	67s 6d	60s	60s 6d
b	70s 6d	73s 6d	72s 6d	65s	65s6d [26]

Note: a, b and c are separate pay rises given in each year

It was shortly after the war that the shipyards and their work force became central to one of the saddest events in the industry's history: the expulsion of thousands of Catholics and non-Unionist Protestants from their jobs. The pre-war crisis on the Home Rule question re-emerged after the 1918 general election, in which Sinn Fein won a majority of seats outside Ulster. The newly elected MPs refused to take their seats in Westminster and instead formed an Irish government which issued a Proclamation of Independence, which to the fury of Ulster's Unionists included the whole country. By July 1920, the situation in the southern counties of Ireland bordered on full-scale war between nationalists and the Royal Irish Constabulary, supported by the British army. Tensions increased in Belfast. On 12 July Edward Carson gave a speech to Orangemen which was somewhat ill-considered, given the sectarian passions within the community.[29] On the 21st of the month, following further deaths in the south and serious rioting in Derry, a meeting of Unionist workers at Workman

Clark's yard developed into what has become known as the 'Belfast Expulsions'.[30] In a letter to the *Dublin Evening Telegraph* of 11 November, James Baird, a member of Belfast City Council – also a Protestant who had been expelled from his workplace – related what had happened:

> Every Roman Catholic – whether ex-serviceman who had proved his loyalty to England during the Great War, or Sinn Feiner who claims to be loyal to Ireland alone – was expelled from the shipyards and other works; … Almost 10,000 workers are at present affected, and on several occasions men have attempted to resume work only to find the 'loyal' men still determined to keep them out. I am informed that one Catholic has been permitted to start on the Queen's Island – one out of thousands, assuming the report is true.[31]

This was not a new experience; Catholics had been expelled on a number of occasions in the past and there had been sectarian problems in the Belfast shipyards from the earliest days of the industry. Edward Harland told the 1886 Riot Commission that he had threatened to close the yard in 1864 to prevent the expulsion of Catholics but that relations were now good within the yard.[32] A police officer told this body that only 500 of the 3,500 employed in the Queen's Island shipyards were Catholic and Harland admitted that only 225 of his 3,000 workers were Catholic.[33] The sensitivity of the shipyard managers to accusations of religious intolerance was increased by the fact that during the 1886 disturbances Catholics had been expelled from the yards.[34] Shipyard workers were conspicuous participants in a number of riots over the years and outbreaks of violence often sectarian violence often began in Workman Clark's yard.[35] During the 1912 Home Rule Crisis 2,400 Catholics and 600 'Rotten Prods' were driven from their places of work by violence or intimidation.[36]

However, the sheer scale of the 1920 outbreak marks it out. Although Catholics were the main focus of attention, it should be remembered that 'rotten prods', whose left wing or anti-Unionist views were seen as treacherous, formed almost a quarter of those expelled.[37]

What was the response of management to these events? William Pirrie tried to resist the expulsion of workers from the yard but his efforts were ineffectual and dismissed as 'quite contemptible' by the main Catholic historian of these events.[38] The expulsions began, as often happened, in the yard of Workman Clark where the management were more overtly Unionist in sympathy.[39] There was little pressure from the trade union movement, only the Amalgamated Society of Carpenters and Joiners called members out on strike to try and force eight firms, including the shipyards, to reinstate expelled workers, but this was largely ignored.[40] Cynically there had also been a marked fall in new orders after the short post-war boom and these events did not disrupt production sufficiently to create a problem for the yards.

At its peak in terms of tonnage produced and prestige of ships built, immediately before the First World War, the shipbuilding industry in Belfast employed over 25,000 men and between 1906 and 1914, an average of just under 10% of the merchant tonnage produced by British yards was launched on the Lagan.[41] So great was the dominance of British shipbuilding in these years that Belfast produced approximately 6% of world output. In 1913, the last full year's production before the outbreak of war, Harland and Wolff launched a modest total of five ships, displacing 62,789 tons. During that year, Workman Clark launched eleven vessels totalling 88,200 tons, a record for the firm.[42] By 1933, however, the industry had changed almost beyond recognition. In that year, Workman Clark delivered only two passenger/cargo ships with a combined tonnage of 13,800.[43] The Belfast yard of Harland and Wolff delivered nothing, although

Workman Clark built the 9,000-ton tanker *Chesapeake* for the Anglo-American Oil Co in 1927. Such ships became important products of the Belfast yards after the First World War. The relative simplicity of such vessels, compared to pre-war liners and cargo-passenger ships, however, resulted in reduced employment in the yards.

the company's yards on the Clyde produced a number of vessels. The labour force in Belfast stood at only 2,573 even this was an increase on the previous year, with most of the yard being on a 'care and maintenance' basis.[44] What caused this speedy and dramatic collapse within the Belfast shipbuilding industry and the consequent high levels of unemployment amongst the skilled working class of Belfast?

In the early post-war years, Workman Clark had appeared to be in a stronger position than Harland and Wolff, but this was to prove to be deceptive. As a result of a huge loan taken out in the company's name by the Northumberland Shipping Co when it acquired Workman Clark in 1920, which was used to repay the parent companies' debts rather than to develop the yard, the firm had become financially unstable.[45] In 1927, the company's credibility was seriously damaged when its directors were prosecuted for issuing a false prospectus at the time of the 1920 takeover.[46] In January 1928, the firm was declared bankrupt and remained closed until March, when a 'management buy-out' by William Strachan, the former company secretary, was successful.[47] The new company, Workman Clark (1928) Ltd, was just beginning establish itself when the demand for shipping collapsed in the wake of the Wall Street Crash. At the end of 1930, Strachan suggested a merger with Harland and Wolff and in November was forced to close the yard temporarily.[48] The position of the yard became increasingly precarious. Disaster struck in November 1931, when a fire seriously damaged the 20,000 ton liner *Bermuda*,

Bermuda, a 20,000-ton motor vessel built for the New York – Bermuda service of Furness Withy and Co, the largest ship ever built by Workman Clark.

which was with the yard for repair. In May 1932, the firm purchased the vessel from the owners, to avoid a damages claim of a million pounds.[49] At the end of the month, Strachan was forced to admit that 'all our slips are empty'.[50] He added further, 'we are neither down-hearted or without hope'. However, the company were unable to cope with worsening conditions and finally succumbed in 1935, when the yard was acquired and closed down by British Shipbuilders Limited.[51]

Harland and Wolff, although appearing to be massively over-extended as a result of pre-war expansion and further burdened with a backward-looking and at times incompetent management which proved unwilling or unable or adapt to the realities of the post-World War One world, was able to survive.[52] David Johnson suggested that the firm's survival was due to a combination of factors. Government support, pre-war investment in new technology, particularly diesel propulsion and the comparative buoyancy of demand for ships of the type the firm specialised in were particularly significant.[53] These factors were important, but do they explain the survival of Harland and Wolff and the failure of Workman Clark? Government assistance, for example, was available to both companies.[54] The question of output is more complex than Johnson suggests, and the survival of the firm depended on the adoption of new products rather than reliance on the established pattern of production (Figures 16 and 17). Harland and Wolff had certainly invested heavily in Burmeister and Wain diesel technology before the war.[55] However, their early motor vessels and their engines were built in the company's Clyde yards rather than in Belfast. The first motor vessel to be built by Harland's in the city was the *Asturias*, launched in July 1925 and delivered in February 1926.[56] Still, Harland's did not enjoy a monopoly of diesel technology and Workman Clark also invested in this new propulsion system, becoming licensees of the Sulzer engine.[57] The first motor vessel built in Belfast was Workman Clark's *Marudu* of 1924–25, built for Alfred Holt and Co.[58] In terms of output and technology, Workman Clark were not much different from Harland and Wolff in the post-war era. Why did one survive and the other collapse? An aspect of this may well have been the more consistent, if not always inspired, management at Harland's compared with the 'wee' yard but it is difficult to avoid the conclusion that they were also simply lucky.

FIGURE 16

Shipbuilding in Belfast 1900–1933 [59]

| | HARLAND AND WOLFF | | WORKMAN CLARK | |
	SHIPS	TONNAGE	SHIPS	TONNAGE
1900–04	33	372,000	53	274,200
1905–09	44	395,930	61	332,800
1910–14	29	365,710	46	359,142
1919–23	43	372,446	50	348,383
1924–28	40	282,665	26	147,739
1929–33	33	299,384	24	161,620

In 1909–13 the Belfast yards produced 9.5% of United Kingdom merchant shipping; in 1922–30 the figure amounted to 9.7% of a much reduced national total. Thus, not only did the Belfast industry survive, it maintained its market share. However, statistics tend to mislead rather than enlighten when looking at shipbuilding at this time. It is necessary to assess the effects of changing world economic conditions and subsequent patterns between the wars. If we look simply at the number of ships launched, the situation does not appear to be overly pessimistic (see Figure 16). Output was reduced but hardly to the degree that might be expected. To compensate for the cyclic nature of the industry, data have been grouped into five-year intervals, thus allowing particularly good years and bad years to counterbalance each other. This method conceals considerable year-on-year variation in output, as the period between 1929 and 1933 demonstrates (see Figure 17). The fortunes of the yards swung violently and this inevitably led to increasing periods of unemployment for workers within the industry. Such variation in output had always been a feature of the British shipbuilding industry,[60] but was the market for Belfast ships more unstable after the war than before? After the short post-war boom, world-wide demand for shipping was reduced to such a degree that established customers of the pre-war period could no longer generate sufficient orders to keep the yards working at full capacity. In the case of Harland and Wolff, the situation was exacerbated by the death of Pirrie in June 1924, for he seems to have been the only person who understood how the 'Commission Club' functioned.[61]

FIGURE 17

Belfast Shipbuilding Output 1929–33 [62]

	HARLAND AND WOLFF		WORKMAN CLARK	
	SHIPS	TONNAGE	SHIPS	TONNAGE
1929	6	41,250	7	53,900
1930	16	130,000	11	54,000
1931	8	76,598	3	33,300
1932	3	50,999	1	5,740
1933	0	0	2	13,800

If we discount the numbers and look rather at the figure for tonnage produced, matters look less healthy (see Figure 16). Fewer ships were being ordered and they were also smaller. This need not necessarily have caused a problem, as the amount of labour needed to construct a ship is not proportionate to the vessel's size; for example, ten times the manpower required to build a 1,000 ton ship is not necessary for the construction of a 10,000 ton vessel. Possibly the most critical factor was the type of ship being built in Belfast in these years. After the war, there was a definite move away from labour-intensive passenger craft towards less complex cargo vessels (see Figure 18). This change in production affected employment within the industry. Passenger ships of all types required a great deal of work at the 'fitting out' stage to make them ready for service. Even the most basic emigrant liner needed cabins, dining rooms, galleys and other domestic features. Conversely, even the most complex of cargo vessels did not require such extensive internal fitting out and employment of many trades was subsequently reduced. An excellent example of this trend was the increasing importance of oil tankers, a type of vessel almost unknown in Belfast's yards prior to the war, when they constituted only 0.8% of Belfast's production between 1900-1913.[63] Such ships were little more than a series of tanks, enclosed within a hull, combined with an engine.

Geary and Johnson point out that tankers increased from 3% to 16% of British merchant tonnage between 1914 and 1938 and that such vessels represented 11% of Belfast's production between 1920 and 1939.[64] Clearly this type became a major element of Belfast's output. However, these figures under represent their importance, as many of the tankers produced were small river or coastal types, with the result that the number of hulls was greater than the percentage of tonnage output suggests. This trend is particularly noticeable in the case of Harland and Wolff, who developed a specialism in shallow draft and coastal tankers in these years.

FIGURE 18

Belfast Shipbuilding: Output of Specific Types [65]

	HARLAND AND WOLFF		WORKMAN CLARK	
	1900–14	1919–33	1900–14	1919–33
Cargo vessels	21.7%	65.8%	47.4%	57.0%
Passenger ships	52.8%	19.9%	6.3%	6.5%
Cargo/passenger	14.2%	7.2%	33.1%	14.9%

FIGURE 19

Production of Oil Tankers in Belfast 1919–1933 [66]

	HARLAND AND WOLFF	WORKMAN CLARK	TOTAL
Total hulls launched	115	100	215
Total tonnage	954,495	657,752	1,612,247
Tanker hulls	34	7	41
Tanker tonnage	110,663	54,260	164,923
% Hulls (tanker)	29.6%	7.0%	19%
% Tonnage (tanker)	11.6%	8.2%	10.2%

The Belfast shipbuilding industry in the inter-war years underwent a painful process of adaptation, as the world market for shipping changed, with the result that Belfast built fewer vessels of smaller size and with much reduced labour. The effects of this change in vessel type were to prove catastrophic for the industry's labour force. At the end of the First World War, the yards provided employment for 36,000 men[67] and the industry was so desperate for labour that wages rose to unprecedented levels. On 27 August 1919 there were 13,897 workers employed in the south yard and 6,160 in Harland's newly established east yard.[68] The Engine works had over 6,000 men in employment in May, and in December there were 1,265 on the 'staff'.[69] The reductions were rapid; by 21 July 1920 there were a mere 12,000 shipyard hands employed in the east and south yards, 924 in the electrical department and 5,800 in the Engine works.[70] On 1 April 1921 the figures for these groups of workers were 10,403, 860 and 5,454.[71] The redundancies continued and over the next five months the work force fell dramatically.[72] Between May and August 1921, Harland and Wolff shed 58% of the shipyard labour and 35% of the Engine shop work force.

The redundancies affected the entire labour force. In 1920, 54.1% of the yard's workers had been skilled men or apprentices and 39% unskilled, with the balance being made up of semi-skilled workers of various types.[73] By July 1921 the figures were 53.9% and 40.2% respectively and of those laid off between April and September, 44.4% were skilled and 48.3% unskilled.[74] By 1932 the yard, according to Moss and Hume, was reduced to operating on a maintenance only basis, employing only foremen and apprentices.[75] In December, their numbers totalled 1,554, a considerable reduction from the 1919 figure of 1,896. Even within this 'secure' group there had been a 20% reduction in employment.[76]

The Belfast shipbuilding industry performed well compared with other regions, but changes in market conditions and reduced levels of demand resulted in serious under-utilisation of capacity and widespread unemployment. At the height of this crisis, after the launching of the 14,000 ton passenger/cargo ship *Highland Patriot* in December 1931, Harland's launched nothing in Belfast until the *Waiwera* of May 1934.[77] If the years between 1900 and 1914 were the golden age of Belfast's shipyards, the early 1930s were their darkest hour.

NOTES

1 Harland and Wolff had built a number of small naval vessels and supplied machinery to the Admiralty. Moss and Hume, *Shipbuilders*, pp. 27, 40, 56, 104, 118, 123, 144. Workman Clark did not build for the Admiralty but carried out repair and refit work. Workman Clark, *Shipbuilders and engineers*, photographic evidence in book.
2 Workman Clark, *Shipbuilding*, p. 52.
3 Ibid., Building List.
4 Moss and Hume, *Shipbuilders*, p. 181.
5 Ibid., pp. 510-19.
6 Ibid, pp. 179, 185, 196.
7 Ibid., pp. 510-19.
8 Workman Clark, *Shipbuilding*, 'Particulars'.
9 Belfast City Council, *The Great War*, p. 123.
10 Ibid., p. 52.
11 Ibid., p. 120.
12 Ibid., p. 122.
13 Ibid., p. 123.
14 Ibid., p. 123.
15 Moss and Hume, *Shipbuilders*, pp. 175-6.
16 Ibid., pp. 179, 185.
17 Ibid., p. 179.
18 Ibid., pp. 175, 180.
19 Ibid., p. 180.
20 Ibid., pp. 186-7.
21 Harland and Wolff Papers, 31/7/1916.
22 Beattie, *People*, p. 119.
23 Harland and Wolff Papers, 25/10/1922.
24 Ibid.
25 Ibid., 1/9/1919.

	TOOL PRICES	
	PRE-WAR	POST-WAR
Stanley Plane No 7	16s 0d	£1 8s 0d
Stanley Plane No 4	9s 0d	£1 1s 0d
Wooden Plane	4s 9d	10s 6d
Set of Chisels	15s 3d	£1 7s 1d
Hand Saw	6s 6d	13s 0d
Tennon Saw	5s 6d	10s 10d

26 Ibid., 1/9/1919 and 9/1919.
27 Ibid., 28/8/ 1917.
28 Kenna, *Belfast pogrom*, p. 32.
29 Morgan, *Labour and Partition*, p. 267.
30 Patterson, *Class conflict and sectarianism*, pp. 115-42.
31 Kenna, *Belfast pogrom*, p. 19.
32 Belfast Riots Commission 1886 [Cd 4925] BPP 1887 XVIII Questions 7582–7597.
33 Ibid., Questions 74. 7585-7594.
34 Gray, *City in revolt*, p. 18.

35 Moss and Hume, *Shipbuilders*, p. 225; Stewart, *Ulster crisis*, pp. 100, 208. Farrell, *Northern Ireland: the Orange State*, pp. 28–9; Johnson, 'Sir George Smith Clark' *Dictionary of National Biography*.

36 Gray, *City in revolt*, p. 212.

37 Morgan, *Labour and Partition*, pp. 269–70.

38 Kenna, *Belfast pogrom*, p. 20.

39 Moss and Hume, *Shipbuilders*, p. 225; Stewart, *Ulster crisis*, pp. 100, 208; Greaves, *James Connolly*, pp. 290–1; Farrell, *Northern Ireland: the Orange State*, pp. 290–1; Johnson, 'Sir George Smith Clark' *Dictionary of National Biography*.

40 Higenbottam, *Our Society's history*, pp. 226–9.

41 Geary and Johnson, 'Shipbuilding', p. 49.

42 Moss and Hume, *Shipbuilders*, pp. 519–20; Workman Clark, *Shipbuilding*, 'Particulars'.

43 Workman Clark, *Shipbuilding*, 'Particulars'.

44 Moss and Hume, *Shipbuilders*, pp. 292, 300.

45 Johnson, *Economy*, pp. 31–2.

46 *Belfast Newsletter*, 28 November 1927; *Belfast Telegraph*, 21 November 1927.

47 *Northern Whig* and *Belfast Post*, 2 March 1928.

48 *Belfast Telegraph*, 28 November 1930; Moss and Hume, *Shipbuilders*, p. 288.

49 *Irish Times* and *Belfast Morning News*, 3 May 1932.

50 *Northern Whig*, *Belfast Post*, 30 May 1932.

51 Johnson, *Economy*, p. 132; Moss and Hume, *Shipbuilders*, pp. 306–7.

52 Moss and Hume, *Shipbuilders*, pp. 291–3.

53 Johnson, *Economy*, p. 132.

54 *Northern Whig*, *Belfast Post*, 13 October 1932.

55 Moss and Hume, *Shipbuilders*, pp. 155, 179, 188, 234.

56 Ibid., p. 521; Pounder, *Engines*, p. 35.

57 Workman Clark, *Shipbuilding*, pp. 44–6.

58 Ibid., 'Particulars'; *Lloyd's Register of Shipping*, 1924–5, 1937–8.

59 Moss and Hume, *Shipbuilders*, pp. 510–9; Workman Clark, *Shipbuilding*, 'Particulars'.

60 Geary and Johnson, 'Shipbuilding', pp. 47–9.

61 Moss and Hume, *Shipbuilders*, pp. 243–4.

62 Ibid.

63 Ibid.

64 Geary and Johnson, 'Shipbuilding', pp. 54, 58.

65 Moss and Hume, *Shipbuilders*, pp. 516–35; Workman Clark, *Shipbuilding*, 'Particulars'.

66 Ibid.

67 *Brown and Nolan's*, p. 60.

68 Harland and Wolff Papers, 27/8/1919.

69 Ibid., 18/6/1919 and 12/12/1919.

70 Ibid., 12/1/1921.

71 Ibid., 1/4/1921.

72 Ibid., 1/4/1921 and 1/9/1921.

73 Ibid., 12/1/1921.

74 Ibid., 20/7/1921 and 6/9/1921.

75 Moss and Hume, *Shipbuilders*, p. 301.

76 Ibid., p. 292; Harland and Wolff Papers, 27/8/1919.

77 Moss and Hume, *Shipbuilders*, p. 535.

5

CONCLUSION

SHIPBUILDING WAS A MOST UNLIKELY SUCCESS STORY in Belfast and its prosperity was created by a strange mixture of entrepreneurial ability, timing, technical expertise and employment patterns. The Belfast shipyards specialised in large merchant vessels, the demand for which was particularly buoyant in the decades before the First World War, as increasing trade and migration created an ever-increasing demand for shipping capacity. Although it has been suggested that the Belfast shipbuilders were over-specialised and too slow to adapt to changing conditions, this was not the case. Belfast's yards were to prove themselves quick to adopt new methods, developing new products such as refrigerated vessels before the war and proving highly adaptable during the conflict. Admittedly, management in both yards could be poor and at times verged on the incompetent, but in neither case was this the main reason for the yards' difficulties.

The major problems faced by Belfast's shipbuilders were not created by their actions or the structure of the industry within the city, but by a massive recession in the world economy in the years between the wars. This caused a reduction in the level of world trade and in particular reduced the flow of emigrants travelling to the United States from Europe. This in turn had the effect of reducing the demand for shipping space and for the large liners and cargo carriers in which Belfast specialised. Given the disadvantages which the region faced compared to other shipbuilding centres, adapting to changing market conditions was particularly problematic for the Belfast yards. Whilst they were successful in moving into new ship types, such as tankers, and new technology, such as motor vessels, this was not enough to save Workman Clark, who faced financial difficulties of a much more serious nature than those of Harland and Wolff. The industry, defined as more than one producer, lasted just over fifty years in Belfast, although Harland and Wolff can argue, with some justice, that they constituted an industry on their own after their rival's closure. At their peak just before and after the First World War, the yards created a huge amount of highly paid work for the male labour force of Belfast. The effect which these workers had on the wider economy was immense. When the yards closed, temporarily or permanently, the working class of Belfast suffered unemployment and poverty of hitherto unknown proportions.

Shipbuilding was the last of the 'main' industries to develop in Belfast but in terms of wealth-creation and prestige, it was perhaps the greatest of the city's employers. Nevertheless, it can be compared to the city's most illustrious creation: the *Titanic*. Like the *Titanic* the industry appeared so stable and secure that none would have believed that it would sink into financial chaos but the iceberg of depressed demand caused it to sink slowly despite valiant efforts to save it. In the case of both the industry and the liner, it can be argued that more could have been done; however, as with the events of that fateful night of 14 April 1912, such knowledge only comes with hindsight. A common denominator between both disasters was perhaps the fact that those on the bottom rung of the social order suffered most, as mass unemployment led to increasing poverty and falling living standards in the inter-war years.

APPENDIX

SHIPBUILDING IN BELFAST 1880 TO 1935

The figures quoted for Harland and Wolff and Workman Clark are fairly complete; those for MacIlwaine and Co. show only larger vessels produced in the yard.

	HARLAND AND WOLFF		WORKMAN CLARK		MacILWAINE & CO.	
	SHIPS	TONNAGE	SHIPS	TONNAGE	SHIPS	TONNAGE
1880	7	11,082	2	800	1	80
1881	7	19,903	5	1800	2	509
1882	7	19,835	5	6000	4	938
1883	10	25,851	8	8900	4	1339
1884	9	22,767	12	9800	3	981
1885	15	31,717	4	7000	1	271
1886	8	19,544	5	8000	1	450
1887	6	13,581	6	3300	3	831
1888	11	40,970	11	10,800	3	2,432
1889	9	39,587	7	18,100	3	3,750
1890	15	62,642	10	15,100	4	2,008
1891	11	51,562	12	21,700	5	2,015
1892	13	70,116	8	22,800	5	4,919
1893	16	61,393	9	19,000	2	4,126
1894	2	64,903	9	33,000	1	541
1895	8	58,299	9	34,100		
1896	9	58,575	12	42.900		
1897	11	82,465	7	25,100		
1898	7	65,645	9	53,900		
1899	7	79,845	7	45,500		
1900	7	81,251	10	56,600		
1901	3	45,737	12	53,100		
1902	8	91,290	12	75,800		
1903	5	72,004	7	44,500		
1904	10	81,718	12	44,200		
1905	7	60,381	12	58,000		
1906	10	75,277	13	65,100		

1907	9	95,920	12	60,900
1908	8	78,834	8	50,600
1909	10	85,518	16	88,200
1910	3	29,560	8	50,100
1911	10	116,963	10	67,600
1912	9	125,952	10	83,600
1913	5	62,789	11	84,700
1914–18	11	Admiralty	36	Admiralty
	26	Merchantmen 286,649	34	Merchantmen 238,600
				+ Barges
1919	11	73,591	13	87,600
1920	14	79,141	13	80,035
1921	4	47,056	13	88,558
1922	6	68,040	6	51,300
1923	7	104,618	5	40,900
1924	4	47,783	9	45,800
1925	4	9,488	7	25,911
1926	5	56,230	3	26,760
1927	14	107,070	6	48,911
1928	13	63,094	1	357
1929	6	41,250	7	53,900
1930	16	130,537	11	54,880
1931	8	76,598	3	33,300
1932	3	50,999	1	5,5740
1933	0	0	2	13,800
1934	4	32,445	3	29,000
1935	7	52,678	1	

POSTSCRIPT

CAN BELFAST'S SHIPYARD SURVIVE? The newspapers are full of stories, which are in turn optimistic and depressing, but on balance I feel the 'unlikely success story' is about to end. What went wrong? The world has changed since the 1870s and the patterns of trade and travel that once generated orders for Belfast's shipyards have long vanished. There may be a return to liner building to meet the needs of a growing cruise market but after years of 'economies' Belfast no longer has the labour force or facilities to build such vessels. It is sad to witness the passing of a great tradition but economics are brutal and accountants heartless – the end is nigh.

BIBLIOGRAPHY

MANUSCRIPT SOURCES

Hanna Bell Papers, Public Record Office of Northern Ireland, BRO 14760

Harland and Wolff Papers, Public Record Office of Northern Ireland, D2805

BRITISH PARLIAMENTARY PAPERS (BPP)

Board of Trade Reports of Strikes and Lockouts 1888–1914

Irish Census, 1861, 1871, 1881, 1891, 1901, 1911

Belfast Riots Commission 1886 BPP 1887 XVIII

Royal Commission on Labour, Third Report, Shipbuilding BPP 1892 XXXII

Statistical tables and charts BPP 1905 LXXXIV

Report of an enquiry by the Board of Trade into working class rents, housing and retail prices BPP 1908 CVII

Report to the Secretary of State for the Home Department on accidents occurring in shipbuilding yards BPP 1913 LX

PUBLISHED SOURCES

BARDON, J., *History of Ulster* (Belfast, Blackstaff, 1992)

BEATTIE, G., *We are the people: journeys through the heart of Protestant Ulster* (London, Mandarin, 1993)

Belfast and Ulster Trades Directory, various dates

BELFAST CITY COUNCIL, *The Great War 1914–18: Ulster greets her faithful sons and remembers her glorious dead* (Belfast, W. & G. Baird, 1919)

Browne and Nolan's illustrated geography: Ireland (Dublin, Browne & Nolan, 1921)

BUDGE, I. and O'LEARY, C., *Belfast approach to crisis: a study of Belfast politics, 1613–1970* (London, Macmillan, 1973)

CLEGG, H.A., FOX, A. and THOMPSON, A.F., *A history of British trade unions since 1889: Vol. 1, 1889–1910* (Oxford, Clarendon Press, 1964)

COATES, K. and TOPHAM, T., *History of the Transport and General Workers' Union* (Oxford, Blackwell, 1991)

COE, W.E., *The engineering industry in the north of Ireland* (Newton Abbott, David & Charles, 1969)

CONNOLLY, J., Collected works (2 vols. Dublin, New Books, 1987 and 1988)

CURTIS, L.P., *Apes and angels: the Irishman in Victorian culture* (Newton Abbott, David & Charles, 1971)

Dictionary of national biography (London, Smith, Elder, 1885–1900)

DOUGAN, D., *History of North East shipbuilding* (London, Allen & Unwin, 1968)

DOUGAN, D., *The shipwrights* (Newcastle upon Tyne, Graham, 1975)

DYOS, H.J. and ALDCROFT, D.W., *British transport* (Leicester, Leicester University Press, 1969)

FARRELL, M., *Northern Ireland: the Orange State* (London, Pluto Press, 1980)

FYRTH, H.J. and COLLINS, H., *The foundry workers* (Manchester, 1959)

GEARY, F. and JOHNSON, W., 'Shipbuilding in Belfast', *Irish Economic and Social History* XVI (1989), pp. 42–64

GRAY, J. *City in revolt: James Larkin and the Belfast Dock Strike of 1907* (Belfast: Blackstaff, 1985)

GREAVES, C.D., *Life and times of James Connolly* (London, Lawrence & Wishart, 1976)

HIGENBOTTAM, S., *Our Society's history* (Manchester, Amalgamated Society of Woodworkers, 1939)

HUGHES, F., *By hand and brain: the story of the Clerical and Administrative Workers' Union* (London, Lawrence & Wishart, 1953)

Industries of Ireland: part 1. Belfast and the towns of the North (London, Historical Publishing Co., 1891)

JEFFERYS, J.B., *The story of the Engineers 1800–1945* (London, Lawrence & Wishart, 1946)

JOHNSON, D., *The interwar economy in Ireland* (Dundalk, Economic &

Social History Society of Ireland, 1985)

KENNA, G.B., *Facts and figures of the Belfast pogrom, 1920–1922* (Dublin, O'Connell Publishing Co.,1922)

KENNEDY, L. and OLLERENSHAW, P., eds. *An economic history of Ulster: 1820–1940* (Manchester, Manchester University Press, 1987)

KIDD, A.T., comp. *History of the tin-plate workers and sheet metal workers and braziers societies* (London, National Union of Sheet Metal Workers and Braziers, 1949)

Lloyd's Register of Shipping, various dates.

LYNCH, J.P., *A tale of three cities: comparative studies in working class life* (London, Macmillan, 1998)

LYNCH, J.P., 'Belfast's third shipyard', *Ulster Folklife*, 41 (1995), pp. 19–25

LYNCH, J.P., 'Belfast shipbuilding industry 1919–1933', *Ulster Folklife*, 43 (1997), pp. 18–25

LYNCH, J.P., 'Harland and Wolff: labour force and industrial relations, autumn 1919', *Saothar* 22 (1997), pp. 47–61

MARSH, A. and RYAN, V., *Historical directory of trade unions* (4 vols. Aldershot, Gower, 1980, 1984, 1987, 1994)

MORGAN, A., *Labour and Partition: the Belfast working class 1905–1923* (London, Pluto Press, 1991)

MORTIMER, J.E., *A history of the Association of Engineering and Shipbuilding Draughtsmen* (London, Association of Engineering and Shipbuilding Draughtsmen, 1960)

MORTIMER, J.E., History of the Boilermakers' Society (2 vols. London, Allen & Unwin, 1973, 1982)

MOSS, M.S. and HUME, J.R., *Shipbuilders to the world: 125 years of Harland and Wolff, Belfast, 1861–1986* (Belfast, Blackstaff, 1986)

MOSS, M.S. and HUME, J.R., *Workshop of the British Empire* (London, Heinemann,1977)

MOSSES, W., *A history of the Pattern Makers' Association*, 1872–1922 (London, United Pattern Makers Association Executive Committee, 1922)

OLIVER, T., *Dangerous trades: the historical, social and legal aspects of industrial occupations as affecting health* (London, E.P. Dutton, 1902)

OWEN, D.J., *History of Belfast* (Belfast, W. & G. Baird, 1921)

PATTERSON, H., *Class conflict and sectarianism: the Protestant working class and the Belfast labour movement 1868–1920* (Belfast, Blackstaff, 1980)

POLLARD, S. and ROBERTSON, P., *The British shipbuilding industry 1870–1914* (Cambridge, Mass, Harvard University Press, 1979)

POUNDER, C.C., *Some notable Belfast-built engines* (Belfast, Belfast Association of Engineers,1948)

SMELLIE, J., *Ship .building and repairing in Dublin* (Glasgow, McCorquodale, 1935)

STEVENS, W.C., *The story of the E.T.U.* (Hayes, Kent, 1953)

STEWART, A.T.Q., *The Ulster crisis* (London, Faber, 1969)

TUCKETT, A., *The Blacksmiths' history* (London, Lawrence & Wishart, 1974)

ULSTER FOLK AND TRANSPORT MUSEUM, *Facsimile of Olympic/Titanic publicity booklet* (Holywood, UFTM, 1983)

VANCE, R., *The Belfast Shipping List*: y/e 31 December 1888 (Belfast, 1889)

WARD-PERKINS, S., *Select guide to trade union records in Dublin* (Dublin, Irish Manuscripts Commission, 1996)

WISE, S.R., *Lifeline of the Confederacy: blockade running during the Civil War* (Columbia, SC, University of South Carolina Press, 1988)

WORKMAN, CLARK & CO., *The shipbuilding and engineering works of Workman Clark and Co, Ltd: shipbuilders and engineers, Belfast, Ireland.* (Belfast, McCaw, Stevenson & Orr, nd)

WORKMAN CLARK, *Shipbuilding at Belfast 1880–1933* (London, Cheltenham, published for Workman Clark (1928) Ltd, 1934)